PADDY BOGSIDE

PADDY DOHERTY

Edited By
Peter Hegarty

Peter Hegarty produces *The Sunday Supplement* on Today FM.
He is the author of a biography of the writer and Republican
Peadar O'Donnell, published by Mercier Press in 1999.

MERCIER PRESS

ACKNOWLEDGEMENTS

It is my pleasure to thank my many friends, whose comments, criticism and encouragement helped bring this book to completion. My wife, Eileen patiently endured my preoccupation with the book, although she has a far better story to tell. Pat Johnston sacrificed her weekends and holidays to type the manuscript.

I dedicate this book to the people of Derry, who defeated an arrogant police force, humbled an intransigent government and, in their generosity, did not take advantage of either, and to my son, Brendan, a former prisoner of war, sentenced to time in Long Kesh on the basis of an uncorroborated statement made by a paid informer.

CONTENTS

CHAPTER 1

My great-grandfather grew up during the famine years of the 1840s. As a young man, he went to work on a farm owned by an absentee landlord on Scalp Mountain in Inishowen. He eventually became the owner of a farm himself. His son, Hugh Doherty – my grandfather – was a horsebreaker by trade, and travelled around Donegal and Derry. He said that there was only one horse he had failed to break, and that was a wild black stallion which roamed the Scalp Mountain. He was very young when he married a woman of the McLaughlin clan. As his trade forced him to move around, his children were born in various parts of the two counties. At the end of the nineteenth century, the family set up home in the Bogside, the district beneath and to the west of the walled city of Derry. The last child, my father, Hugh 'Scalper' Doherty, was born in 1893. He inherited the moniker from his father; it distinguished him from the many others who bore the same surname, and identified him with the mountain his family hailed from. The family was well settled in the Bogside by 1921, when the English partitioned Ireland. The city of Derry, cut off from its hinterland – Donegal and Inishowen – was now a frontier town, the baleful border no more than five miles from its centre.

The elder 'Scalper' was showing signs of wear and tear after a life of long days and wet nights on the mountains of Inishowen. All of his daughters had married. To him they were no longer part of the clan: he had grandsons called Hillen, but none called Doherty. His eldest son Pat had gone off to America and married, but had no children. People said 'she' was to blame. James, who had followed the cattle trade all his life, was careful of his appearance: his brown boots went with his tweed suit, the carnation he always wore in his buttonhole matched the colour of his cheek. The silk scarf tucked into the collar of his shirt gave him a slightly foppish air, which belied the strength of his 6'2" frame. The old man invested a great deal of hope in him, and expected him to produce children. But he never had a relationship with a woman, although he was never short of offers.

The third son, John, married and had three beautiful daughters. When his wife died, his sister Annie, who had lost her husband in the Great War, took over the rearing of them. John became a chauffeur to a local doctor. He was treated like a lord by the four women in his life, and he never courted or married again. The youngest son, Hugh, my father, was the only one who had been born in Derry, under the shadow of the walled city. He was a small but powerful man. When he stripped on the football field his body looked as if it had been sculpted from marble. He could trail his coat in any company and few dared to cross him. He was like the black stallion his father failed to break on the Scalp Mountain, and the old man wondered if a young girl fresh up from the south would eventually tame him and produce a son to continue his line. My grandfather was still wondering when he died.

The girl from the south, Dora Redmond, had come to Derry to visit her sister, who had married a native of Derry while he was serving with the British army in Wexford during the Great War. The visit lasted several weeks and, before she returned to Wexford, she agreed to marry the youngest son of the man from the Scalp Mountain. The wedding was arranged in secret and the place chosen for the ceremony was Maynooth in County Kildare. No member of her family attended it: she packed her bags in the middle of the night and left home without telling anyone. Hugh Doherty travelled from Derry with the rest of the wedding party, which numbered four. After the wedding, the couple returned to the Bogside, to a tiny, crowded house no more than a stone's throw from the house where he had been born. Later, after his parents passed on, he returned to that house. Their first son was stillborn. As he had died before being baptised, he was destined for Limbo, the place in which – so the Church taught – all who died without the comfort of baptism would forever dwell. Those who died unbaptised would never enter Heaven, nor see the face of God. The only solace the theologians offered my mother, after she had endured nine months of pain, then the anguish of a stillbirth, was the teaching that souls in Limbo would never suffer punishment. The theologians who came up with the concept of Limbo were certainly not divinely inspired. Eighteen months later the local midwife delivered Hugh alive and well in the one-storey attic house in a dog-legged street in the Bogside. Of all of the children, he would be closest to our mother.

Unusually for the Doherty family, my mother gave birth to three sons in a row. Although the first was stillborn, the next two survived to carry on the name. The eldest had the traditional family name of Hugh. I was named Patrick in memory of my uncle, who had died without issue in America. The arrival of two daughters restored the gender balance. Eventually there would be seven girls and four boys. As my birth in 1926 coincided with the Lincoln, an English race, my father put a bet on a horse called Second Edition, which was an also-ran. He should have paid more attention to the jockeys' names: Patrick Donohue rode the winning horse. Ian Paisley was born fourteen days after me, in the cathedral city of Armagh.

Our street was overshadowed by St Eugene's Cathedral. Ladders led up to the attics on one side of the street. The houses on the other side had steep, twisting staircases, which cut into the back rooms at the rear, leaving room for a single bed only.

Our back room held a double bed, where my parents slept. The ladder led to the attic, which was divided in two by a curtain; the boys slept on one side, the girls on the other. The exposed, roughly squared purlin supported the roof. Our clothes hung on four-inch nails hammered in at regular intervals along the length of the purlin. Several makeshift shelves kept the floor free of the clutter accumulated by children as they grow up.

My most vivid memory from my early childhood is of dozens of women on their knees, praying in the kitchen, hallway and out in the street, while my anxious father stood in the backyard, being comforted by another group of women. My mother was having a difficult labour and the neighbours were rallying to her. I was transfixed for a while by the activity. Then I wandered unnoticed from the kitchen to the yard, and into the street, suddenly feeling abandoned and confused. I had felt this way before and these were familiar scenes. Every new arrival in the family made it more difficult for me to maintain my close relationship with my mother. But there were other women in my life. My cousin Rose-Ann, Kathleen across the street, Jean who lived in the corner house and, most important of all, the nun who was my teacher at the convent school. I could barely see her face behind the veil when, at the age of three, I joined her class, but it was love at first sight. My love affair with my teacher lasted a whole year and I believed that she was as committed to me as I was to her. I desperately wanted to remain in her class. But she betrayed me. I well remember the day she and the head nun sat reviewing the whole class. This one was to go to Miss Doherty's class, this one to Miss Durnin, this one to remain for another year with his present teacher. When my name came up, without hesitation the love of my life said, 'Patrick to Miss Doherty.' I was devastated.

From an early age my brother Hugh loved animals. He doted on a succession of canaries, turtles, rabbits, pigeons, Kerry Blue terriers and greyhounds during his childhood years. But he had an incredible hatred of cats, which lingered well into adulthood. He conducted a relentless vendetta against the species and never went to help any cat unfortunate enough to stray into the backyard domain of his favourite Kerry Blue. I believe that this animus stemmed from a horrifying incident during his childhood. I can still clearly recall hearing his cries of anguish when he saw a cat stealing into his pigeon loft. The terrified pigeons flapped around within the confines of the loft, the cat leaping and striking them down as they struggled to escape. My father raced to the loft, but in his agitation he couldn't get the door open. I stood paralysed with shock. Hugh screamed until he shook. Eventually they got the door open, whereupon the cat shot out through my father's legs. Blood dripping from its mouth, it scaled the backyard wall in a flash and disappeared. Of fourteen birds, only six remained alive, some bearing marks left by the marauding cat. Hugh nursed every injured bird back to health and for weeks mourned the loss of the dead ones. Hugh must have been no more than six years old when he began to look after the children who came after him; as he grew older he washed dishes, scrubbed floors and, when my mother was ill, did the shopping. He was the apple of my mother's eye and I didn't like that one bit.

When I was old enough to hunt through the shelves in the attic bedroom, I came upon a revolver and five rounds of ammunition. Ken Maynard was my cowboy hero and I regularly practised a fast-draw, twirling the revolver around my fingers and squinting down its sights at imaginary Indians. It wasn't long before I learned to load the shining bullets. I wondered why the cowboys called theirs six-guns, when mine had only five chambers. I reversed the gun to look into the deep black circular hole and toyed with the idea of squeezing the trigger, but was afraid the noise would betray my knowledge of the secret weapon and end my battles with the Indians.

Work was usually scarce in Derry, but the docks sometimes provided a safety net for the men of the Bogside. Periods of plenty alternated with times of dire hardship: 'Merry and miserable may you be, as long as you work at Derry Quay' was a saying dubiously attributed to Saint Colmcille. Catholic men – merry, miserable or whatever – controlled the docklands and developed the capacity to strangle Derry's industry and commerce, which were dominated by unionist families who zealously guarded their privileged status. Although all of our lives had been shaped by recent momentous political events, Bogsiders only rarely discussed politics. They considered the Treaty, which had formalised the division of the country, to have been an abomination; a united Ireland was the holy grail. My introduction to Anglo-Irish relations came at the dinner table, when it was announced on the radio that the Right Honourable Lloyd George had been admitted to hospital. My father slowly put down his knife and fork and said, in a voice quavering with emotion, 'Hell will never be full until the Welsh bastard is in it.'

Such was the solemn grace said by Hugh, son of Hugh, son of Hugh, and by then father of Hugh, Patrick, Nellie and Jean. The year was 1932. I mention these names because for legal reasons my father requested a copy of his marriage certificate from the Church that year. With disbelief he read the curt reply to his letter, which stated that no marriage between the parties named had taken place in or around the stated date. He asked Father John O'Doherty, the old curate at St Eugene's Cathedral, for help. Father John was one of the few people who had retained the 'O' in front of his surname. He was also a fluent speaker of Irish, and a living symbol of the bond between the Catholic Church and the native Irish. After many letters of enquiry the awful truth emerged. The priest who had conducted the marriage had been a visitor to the parish and had neglected to fill in the appropriate form. The union, duly solemnised before God, had gone unrecorded by Church and State. At the age of six, I was unaware of the crisis besetting the family. As an object of reverence, our parents' wedding photograph was second only to the picture of the Sacred Heart above the mantelpiece. After a long, wearisome series of approaches to church bureaucrats, my parents finally obtained the papal decree which recognised the marriage and legitimised the children. The successful outcome reflected my mother's strength of character and determination, qualities which would stand to her as she settled down to life in the strange, claustrophobic Bogside.

The wooden shutter which covered the only front window of our home had been made and fixed during the curfew imposed on the area by the British army during the Anglo-Irish war of 1920-1 and had never been removed. At the age of seven, I tried to capture some of the drama of that period as I drew the house where I lived in response to the teacher's request. Stories of soldiers in battledress, flat tin helmets and fixed bayonets smashing windows from which the light streamed – making them targets for snipers – were still being told around firesides in the evening. It wasn't easy to recapture history second-hand, but I faithfully reproduced the one-storey building, with the shutter held back to expose the neatly curtained window and the door with its knocker, doorknob and proud number 20. The line of the eave gutter was only about three feet above the door. As I added the roof, with its individual slates, my confidence grew. With a final flourish, I simulated smoke pouring from the chimney. On the days when the Orangemen celebrated their victories, high on the walls of the citadel on the hill, thick black smoke from burning boots and rags poured from chimneys in the Bogside. Sometimes the courts punished these attempts to discommode the Orangemen by imposing fines on the basis of a 200-year-old law. My satisfaction was short-lived. The teacher, leaning over my shoulder, said with exasperation, 'Where did you ever see a house like that?' The reality of my existence was swiftly extinguished, as the teacher's pencil, in bold strokes, sketched a second storey with windows. I never took much of an interest in art after that incident.

To the delight of my parents, I was selected by another, more gentle teacher to serve as an altar boy in the cathedral. Over the years I assisted in the burial of one bishop and helped consecrate another. I was at the bishop's side, holding his crozier, while he ordained priests and celebrated High Mass. I assisted both local and foreign priests and listened to them intone Latin phrases which I barely understood. My favourite experience, however, was helping to solemnise marriages, at which it was the custom for the groomsman to reward the young servers. We'd line up to get our sixpences after the ceremony, but the occasional 'big hitter' might go as high as a half-crown. There were eight of these to a pound in those days. With whatever I had earned, I would run home as fast as I could, the coins in my tightly clenched fist. Sixpence I could keep, but anything more than that I had to share with my mother: two to her and one to me. Young as I was, I was acutely aware of her struggle to make ends meet, and I took pride in occasionally being able to contribute to the family income.

My period of association with the Church was a formative time. I learned discipline and developed a sense of identity. On some matters I have never seen eye to eye with the clergy. I never met an Irish Catholic priest who did not despise the Northern Ireland establishment, but very few of them had any time for the Republican movement either. The Republicans' stated aim was the destruction of the northern statelet and the reunification of Ireland. I was convinced that the clergy were motivated by something other than simple detestation of physical-force Republicanism. They suspected, I believe, that the Republicans were working to a secret socialist agenda. Socialism would pose a challenge to the authority of the Church. My loyalty to the Church was sorely tested at election-time, when priests would drive around the area with the name of the moderate Nationalist candidate displayed on their car windows. My father always voted for the Republican candidate, and appeared to have no difficulty in separating his religion from his politics. In any contest between my father and the Church, I backed my father.

It was Saturday. The ritual of bathing the children in front of the open fire was over and the large zinc bath had returned to its hook on the backyard wall. The ironing was the final chore of the week. My mother kept glancing at the clock on the mantelpiece as she propelled the bow of the cast-iron, gas-fuelled smoother over our Sunday-best clothes. As the hands moved towards ten o'clock, I knew she was getting worried. Where was my father? His workmates who serviced the Liverpool steamer had returned home hours ago. He was usually about an hour behind the rest, as he had the job of releasing the moorings which bound the ship to the dockside. 'Casting off', it was called, and he got an extra two shillings for his efforts. But the ship had sailed hours ago. Where was he now? My mother worked for another hour and then she stood the smoothing iron on its rear end, turned off the gas and said to me, 'We must go and find your father.'

We walked towards the docks, scanning the faces of approaching men. No sign of him. Out of the darkness stepped two policemen. 'Where are you going, ma'am?' one asked.

'I'm looking for my husband. He works at the Liverpool boat and he hasn't returned home.'

The policeman glanced at his companion. Their silent communication heightened our anxiety, and the policeman's next remark did nothing to dispel it. In a gentle tone, he said, 'There has been some trouble down at the docks and you should return home. I think your husband will be all right.' We did not sleep that night. At about ten o'clock the next morning, my father arrived home, heavily intoxicated. He was so drunk that he could neither see, hear nor speak; he must have had the instincts of a homing pigeon to make his way to the house. With difficulty, we got him upstairs to bed; he was virtually unconscious for the next twelve hours. As the day wore on, we began hearing reports that two policemen had been shot at the docks. We waited with apprehension for my father to emerge from his drunken stupor. Over the next two days, delirious shouts emanated from the bedroom, as my father relived the horror he had witnessed. On the third day he emerged, unshaven, red-eyed but reasonably articulate, to tell his story. 'I was with Sammy Gallagher, releasing the ship. He was at one end, me at the other. Just as my rope slapped into the water and was being pulled on board, I heard an argument in the shed behind me.'

Two uniformed policemen – one a constable, the other an officer – were confronting each other. The constable, a big, portly, affable man who was popular with the dockers, must have been caught resting himself on some bales of merchandise. The officer, a smaller, leaner man, was roundly and mercilessly abusing him. He had no sympathy for the constable, who had spent a long time on duty on a very warm day. It wasn't the first time that the officer had publicly rebuked the constable: even the sight of a loosened tunic-collar was enough to send him into a rage. But this time would be the last. My father described what happened next. 'I stood mesmerised as the constable drew his revolver from its holster and shot the officer at point-blank range, and then, placing his left hand on his own right shoulder, he rested the revolver on the crook of his elbow. I rushed forward to try and stop him, but the gun went off, and I saw the side of his head disintegrate as the bullet pierced his skull.'

When my father was finished talking, he fell silent, and spoke no more that day. It was a harrowing time for the whole family, as my father tried to come to terms with what had happened. He gave up working for a time, trying to find some relief in alcohol, dreading the pending inquest, when he would be forced to relive the nightmare on the witness-stand. Some time later, the mystery of his absence that night was clarified. When the police arrived at the scene of the shooting, my father was taken to the barracks, where he waited until he was questioned; he was eventually made to sign a statement. By this time, dawn was breaking. The policemen took him and Sammy Gallagher to a pub in Fountain Street, where they woke the owner and told him to open up. To his dying day, my father never knew who had footed the bill that morning.

Chapter 2

As I came within sight of the ancient fort called Grianan on the hill of Aileach, I felt overawed at its size and air of mystery. The stories concerning Grianan are legion. It was the mythical place where generations of ancient Irish warriors lay entombed, awaiting the call to arise and free Ireland. The Druids had used it to conduct blood sacrifices. The High Kings of Tara had to visit Grianan to receive the submission of the northern chieftains, before their overlordship was formally recognised. The ancient Greek geographer Ptolemy knew of its existence and marked it on his map of the world. I thought about these stories as I slaked my thirst at the holy well and wondered if I could scale the massive walls of the fort – something which only the most adventurous of my friends at school could boast about. I didn't climb them, but I did accept a challenge to visit the 'wishing-chair' deep within the walls. I clambered through the tiny opening at the base of the wall and felt my way along the narrow passage. Halfway along, the passage curved inwards. Suddenly I was in darkness.

I struggled to contain my panic. I steadied myself and continued probing my way along the passage. Finally I got to the end. My hands explored the stones. I found the flat slab which formed the seat of the wishing-chair. I turned myself carefully in the blackness of the tunnel and sat down. I didn't make a wish, but sitting there in silence I felt a strange peace come over me, as if I had arrived home after a long absence. I was late getting home to the Bogside. When I did, my mother began her usual ritual of questioning me about where I had been and who I had been with. I could never understand her concern. 'I warned you,' she would say. 'You are not to be in the company of that family.' I couldn't understand my mother's anger. 'Why not? Why not?' I wanted to scream, but the look on her face silenced me.

Words such as malnutrition, rickets or consumption didn't mean anything to me at the age of eleven. My young friends had a delicate, dark beauty about them. When we swam together in the old disused reservoir, I watched their ribs strain against their sallow skin. They reminded me of my uncle Mick's greyhounds when he had them trained to perfection for an important race. A diet of meat and eggs, and plenty of walking, was all a well-bred greyhound needed. As my friends wasted away before my eyes, it dawned on me that nothing could save them from a early death.

Consumption, as tuberculosis was then called, was rife at the time. Almost half of the young people who died in Northern Ireland in 1937 died of TB. It was a disease of the poor, who lived in cramped and overcrowded conditions. Those who died had often already been weakened by ill-health, bronchitis and diets which wouldn't have sustained greyhounds. Those who survived tended to be inches shorter and pounds lighter than middle-class children in England. The government made some gestures towards alleviating the abject poverty of the working classes. Bowls of soup costing a halfpenny were served at lunchtime in the schools, and senior pupils helped to distribute a free spoonful of cod-liver oil every morning. As my awareness increased, I realised that my mother's face had expressed fear, not anger. She was afraid that someone's touch, caress or kiss would infect one of her children, and feared that our healthy diet – home-baked bread, fat brown eggs straight from the nest, cut-price pork, milk in white enamel cans fresh from the creamery and butter churned in Inishowen homes and smuggled across the border in wicker baskets – would not protect us.

Before home economics became a fashionable subject in schools and colleges, she squeezed a dock-labourer's wages until they screamed. I never knew anyone who could drive a harder bargain in the marketplace. She had lost one child at birth, and by God she would not lose another. In working-class homes in Derry, there was never enough money to last out the week. Friday was payday. Long before it came around, the last pay packet was spent. A network of pawn shops, credit companies and loan sharks tided people over. I hated the pawn shops, with their three brass balls hanging high above the entrance doors. Pawnbroking was the brainchild of a pope who believed that temporarily surrendering something of value for cash was more dignified than begging and that pawnbroking was not tainted by the sin of loaning money for profit. But seeing your father's one and only Sunday suit spread out for inspection on the hardwood counter was a belittling experience. Stains would reduce the pittance the pawnbroker paid to store my father's suit, in anticipation of its redemption in time for Sunday Mass. The service pawnbrokers provided – handling and storing items and keeping them easily accessible – was their defence against accusations of usury. On Saturday evenings, women and children crushed in to redeem their good clothes, which were numbered, wrapped in brown paper parcels and stacked in deep shelves. Pawn shops were the preserves of women and children. Only occasionally would men, down on their luck or looking for the price of a cure after a hard bout of drinking, venture in. The shrewd broker behind the counter would look hard at the item they offered him, and pay out less than he usually would, knowing that he might be obliged to sell to recover his payment, if the item pledged were not reclaimed. Experience had taught pawnbrokers never to trust men who drank. But drunk or sober, the women always honoured their commitments.

To me, Derry was a city of women. They gave it character and bustle as they streamed to and from the shirt factories scattered around the city walls. They took their work home, where they sheared threads from collars to earn a few extra pence. In the evenings, released from work by the factory horns, they filled the cinemas and dance halls. They prided themselves on making the finest shirts in the world. They married early and would temporarily stop making shirts to produce the next generation of stitchers, cuffers, button-holers and collar-makers. They were the colour in a community of grey, unemployed men. Their passion for clothes sustained a network of credit houses and their agents all year round, and climaxed in a magnificent fashion parade as the annual religious retreat came to a close in May. At one retreat I recall the unemployed men, their drabness relieved by white flowers in their buttonholes, loudly renouncing 'the world, the flesh and the devil', prompted by a visiting missionary who preached about 'an honest day's pay for an honest day's work'.

The shirt factories employed young and old women. They related easily to each other at work and outside. The unemployed men were starved of social interaction. Drink was their scourge; they consumed great quantities of alcohol during long hours of apathetic maundering in men-only stand-up bars. Men asserted their traditional dominance over women, who had to put up with them as best they could. Few women had more on their plates than a friend of ours who lived nearby. She was a handsome, amply built woman. But for all her bulk, she could skip with the best of the youngsters in the street, and often did. She had a sharp tongue, and a sense of humour to lighten the heaviest load. I was very fond of this light-footed and lighter-hearted extrovert, who always addressed me as 'Doherty' and never used my Christian name. Her life was tough. She was trying to rear a family in hard times, with a husband addicted to drink. Other women were in the same boat – poverty seemed to scour their very souls – but none had her ability to cope or her caustic wit. She dreaded weekends and would count her blessings if he came home so drunk that he only desired sleep. The worst times were when he had no money to buy his favourite antidote to boredom – a cheap wine known locally as 'Red Biddy'. He would come home and wreck the place. He once pulled the dresser to the floor, smashing all the delft – simple, refined pieces of crockery that relieved the monotony of poverty – to pieces on the floor. During one particularly venomous spree, he took the huge pot of potatoes she had cooked for the family's dinner and danced a devil's hornpipe on it, showering crushed potatoes over what furniture remained. They were an extreme case, but a number of marriages were under strain because of the man's sense of frustration. Some couples broke up, but most kept their troubles to themselves and trusted in time as a healer. Infidelity was the only wound that would never heal. That so many marriages survived was a testament to the power of the Church, and even more so to the emotional strength of the women.

After one particularly violent episode, my friend and her children went to a neighbour's house for the night. She returned on her own late the following morning to start the thankless task of rescuing the few unbroken dishes from the mass of broken crockery. She was interrupted by a knock on the door. Her visitors were a pair of nuns who wanted to know why the two youngest girls had not been to ten o'clock Mass that morning. Slightly taken aback by the unexpected arrival of the nuns, she invited them in to inspect the results of her husband's drinking, trusting that they would then understand why her daughters had missed Mass. Surveying the destruction, the younger of the two nuns, in a naive attempt to pour oil on troubled waters, began to recite some excuses for male misbehaviour. My friend responded by tearing into men in general, and in particular the beast who was sleeping off his hangover in the next room. For some inexplicable reason, the young nun replied, 'Don't be too hard on him. Sure, Christ was a man.' My friend, now totally exasperated, shocked the representatives of Mother Church with the words: 'If he was anything like that bastard lying drunk next door, it's no wonder they crucified him.' When she told me the story, she ended it by saying, 'Och! Sure God knows I didn't mean Christ any harm.' Perhaps Christ took pity on her. Some time later the husband banged his head against something. As a result of the accident, his personality completely changed. A mild manner replaced his vile temper and he lost his craving for alcohol.

The close watch the nuns kept on the young was one aspect of the tight hold the Church had on the Catholic community in Derry. It forbade us to mix socially with other Christians. No one suspected that a member of a well-known republican family would challenge the taboos. She was sparkling company, petite, dark and very beautiful, and had set many hearts aflutter. She caused a great stir when she married a Protestant. The rigorous sanctions employed against Catholics who married outside the Church were brought to bear on the teenager, who had answered the call of her heart. At each Mass on Sunday, her name was read out and that most awful punishment – excommunication – was pronounced. I heard the terse statement which severed the limb from the body of the Church. It wasn't the sharp, clean cut of the guillotine, but a blow from a blunt, rusted axe, which mutilated a follower of Christ. I secretly admired the girl for her courage and hoped in my heart that she would find happiness, then immediately felt guilty for harbouring such thoughts. Not for the first time, my heart and head were moving in different directions. I offered a silent prayer that God would understand my ambivalence.

We soon grew too numerous for the small attic-bedroomed house in the Bogside and went to live on the Isle of Derry, where the walled city was only yards from the front door of our new home in Orchard Street. I left here every morning to go to work on the aerodromes which were built outside Derry during the Battle of the Atlantic. From my bedroom window I watched the local cinema, the Opera House, burn to the ground after the owner disregarded an IRA warning not to show Movietone News, a British propaganda newsreel. Britain was not so preoccupied with its war in Europe as to ignore well-known Republicans like Tommy Mellon and Seán Keenan, who – with many others – spent the war years interned without charge or trial under the provisions of the Special Powers Act. While they were denied their freedom, the Apprentice Boys of Derry and the Orange Order were prevented from holding their traditional marches. The authorities feared that the thousands of able-bodied brethren who had refused to answer England's call in her hour of need would be exposed to public ridicule. Many had taken the soft option and joined the B-Specials or the Home Guard instead. Of the 800 local members of the Territorial Army, recruited just before the war started, only 200 were Protestants. Basil McFarland, son of Sir John, a local grandee, proudly led the troops. He tried to buy himself out of the army when he discovered that the territory he had joined to defend included the sand dunes of the Sahara Desert.

The aerodromes completed, I packed my tools to work on London's bombed-out buildings. Suddenly I felt grown up. Two years later I returned to Derry, with a great admiration for the fighting spirit of the English people and an appreciation of British military power. I understood now why my father had cursed Lloyd George, the former Prime Minister of Britain, who had threatened 'immediate and terrible war' if the Irish negotiators did not accept the conditions laid down in the Anglo-Irish Treaty of 1921. Having seen the indescribable destruction the war had visited on London, I now understood what 'terrible war' meant. If Lloyd George had had something similar in mind for Ireland, then my father had every right to hate him.

I returned with enough money to start making arrangements to marry Eileen McDaid, for whom I had carried a torch since I was sixteen years old. I discussed my plans with my close friend, Donal McCafferty. We agreed that we could double my savings by backing the last two favourites at a greyhound meeting. Needless to say, both dogs were also-rans. I had to pack my bags for England again. Three months later I was back to continue the wedding arrangements, having vowed never to gamble again.

Finding a house proved impossible. The lack of accommodation was so chronic that most houses were occupied by several families. In fact, it was not uncommon to find entire families living in one room. After the US army departed an encampment at Springtown, on the western edge of the city, many families occupied the corrugated Nissan huts left behind. They were so desperate that the cold, draughty, dark, semi-circular metal huts, built years before as a transit camp for military personnel, were worth fighting for. Wrong-footed by the people, the government finally gave in and agreed that the huts could be used as housing. This was the very first initiative to alleviate the deplorable conditions in which most citizens lived. I found work refurbishing the huts. The exodus of people from the city eased the pressure on space there. I was able to find a room for Eileen and me, just three days before our wedding.

We enjoyed our honeymoon in Dublin, knowing that we would have somewhere to return to. Although I had been earning my own living for a number of years and had spent two of these working in England, I was still a boy in a large family, answerable to my parents and subject to family discipline. Now married, I was a Doherty in my own right.

CHAPTER 3

Early in 1959, I fixed two metal numbers, a 1 and a 0, to the door of our new house in Westland Street and started digging up the small front garden, which was filled with the rubble left over from the building work. As the sharp blade of my spade exposed the half-bricks and general debris, I experienced a feeling of satisfaction. I had worked evenings and weekends for two years; against all the odds, I now had a house. I smugly felt that if other Catholics put as much effort into sorting out their problems as I had, we could transform society. As I glanced over the garden area to calculate the amount of topsoil I would need, I was greeted by a tall young man. He introduced himself as John Hume. He was well-built, with thick, wavy black hair. A dimple on his chin gave him a boyish appearance. In some extraordinary way, my thoughts seemed to have found a ready echo in the young stranger's mind. He said he had come to discuss the grim conditions in which the Catholic population was living and its utter inability to effect any change in those conditions. Our encounter was the first of many which prepared the young man for a career in politics. Hume was a teacher of French and the son of a trade-union activist. He had recently abandoned his studies for the priesthood at Maynooth. Only a generation earlier, he would have been unfairly branded 'a failed priest' and people would have whispered about an inability to remain celibate. The gossips had driven many a young man out of his home town. Celibacy evidently ranked above integrity at the time. But a wind of change was already blowing through the universal Church. Here and there, priests were challenging the conservative nature of the Church, and many people were criticising the dominance of dogma over spirituality. Chance had put him in the right place at the right time. I had never come across anyone so young with such confidence in his own ability. We discussed social, political and economic issues into the early hours. In particular we talked about the apathy wasting the Catholic population of Northern Ireland, and especially Derry. We explored the role of the Nationalist Party, concluding that it was no help to the people and would have to be confronted. What we needed were leaders who demanded effort and idealism from the people themselves. We needed leaders who would provide opportunities for people to come together to discuss and solve their problems; who would give them pride in their own achievements, and a sense of power. This 'up by your own bootstraps' philosophy would dominate my own thinking for many years.

Except for a short period during the Second World War, unemployment was endemic to Derry and ran at four times the British average. The city had the highest birth rate in Europe. The number of births every year was roughly the same as the number who left annually for the building sites of England and beyond. Catholics and Nationalists – the terms were as good as synonymous – were helpless because they were politically powerless. Only once in the history of the state had a Nationalist MP been successful in having a bill passed in the Northern Ireland Parliament. It concerned the protection of wild birds. Hume and I shared a common vision of a politicised Catholic community. Paddy Joe Doherty, Seamus Bonner and John Patton, all young teachers, joined our nightly brainstorming sessions, in which we struggled to find an antidote to apathy. Slowly but surely, we drew closer to the understanding that no one was going to help us and that the push for change would have to come from within the Catholic ghettos themselves. We reposed no hope in the Nationalist Party, under the leadership of Eddie McAteer, which, under protest, participated in the Northern Irish political system, propping up the status quo and the Unionist Party. Its supporters seemed content enough with things as they were.

We didn't expect much from the Church either. It provided and maintained the schools, which were bursting at the seams with the physical evidence of a spiralling birth rate. On Sunday mornings, when Mass was celebrated on the hour from seven o'clock to twelve o'clock, the churches were full to overflowing. While the Church passionately defended its role in education, it was generally silent on social and political issues. The people – through bingo sessions, dances and raffles – supported the Church's building programme. With a few individual exceptions, the clergy confined itself to serving the spiritual needs of its flock. The people, then, were like a becalmed ship.

In Derry, the corporation house-building programme had been interrupted for political reasons. The local-authority franchise was restricted to owners of property and householders. The rateable value of his property determined how many votes an owner had. Children living at home, regardless of their age, had no vote. People living in furnished or unfurnished rooms were also denied the vote. There was a logic to all of this. If houses were built, the tenants would automatically qualify for the vote. The people without homes were Catholic and nationalist. To give a Catholic a house also meant giving him the vote. If he didn't have a job either, he was a burden on the rates and social services. If you kept him out of work and refused to house him, he might take his family to live somewhere else, as many did. The right to vote and work, and to live in proper housing – things people take for granted in a normal, democratic society – was denied in Northern Ireland by a ruling class which, forty years earlier, had refused to accept the democratically expressed wishes of the majority of the Irish people. Forty years is a long time: the institutions of the new state were well established by now and reinforced by privilege and prejudice.

For Catholics, this was how it would always be, or so it seemed. But, as is the case always and everywhere, there were people who wouldn't lie down. Cantankerous, loveable Jack Melaugh, a builder and founder member of the Colmcille Debating Society, was someone special. 'The Northern Ireland Government has cut a rod to beat itself by introducing the 1947 Education Act,' he told me. The Act had opened up third-level education to all who were academically suited to it. He pushed the new generation of educated Catholics into the wind, challenging them to stretch themselves in a range of activities, particularly debates at the Colmcille Debating Society, which would prepare them for roles as leaders of the community. 'Our people can't get off their knees unless they can have access to money,' I told Melaugh. 'Without it, we can't build houses or create jobs. Money means power. We need our own bank,' I said.

'See Tony Mulvey. He knows of a system of banking in America which is run by ordinary people,' Melaugh answered.

Father Anthony Mulvey was the clerical equivalent of Melaugh. He stood out among his fellow priests in that he directly involved himself in social problems. He mentioned a woman called Nora Herlihy as a person who understood the American credit-union system well. Hume was instructed to write to her. Nora Herlihy's reply was the most exciting and hopeful thing I had read in decades. Her words seemed to jump out of the pages and shake me. Within months – and against legal advice – I had persuaded our study group to start a credit union. Nine pounds and seven shillings was the sum total of the first night's savings, including membership fees. Eileen became the first female member. Dr Jim Cosgrove was elected President and John Hume, Treasurer. Hume and I worked ceaselessly in double harness to spread the message of credit unionism.

Although we agreed on many issues, there were certain fundamental differences between us. John believed that a more generous and cooperative approach to the authorities by what he called 'an enlightened leadership' was a prerequisite for change. I, on the other hand, was convinced that only after complete removal of British administration would the people of Northern Ireland overcome their divisions – divisions which had been carefully nurtured for political ends. During our discussions it became obvious to me that Hume's idea of 'enlightened leadership' tended towards the premise that John Hume would lead. Despite my misgivings about him, I decided to back Hume, considering him to be the best leader the Catholic people had. His dogged determination and hard work would eventually earn him a Nobel Prize and the title of the greatest Irishman of the twentieth century. While I was a fervent nationalist who believed passionately in a united Ireland, Hume derided the Republic and declared that 'it would always bear the mark of Cain for refusing to go to war on the side of Britain against Nazi Germany.' This was a reference to Ireland's neutrality during the 1939–45 war. I had lived through that period and felt that Ireland's refusal to bow to threats from any of the belligerent powers was her finest hour. De Valera, who had been Taoiseach at the time, was a hero of mine. I will never forget his masterly answer to Winston Churchill after the war, when Churchill, flushed with victory, attacked Ireland's neutrality. De Valera's reply was utterly dignified. I remember his voice rising and falling, as the old wireless crackled with static:

> Could he not find in his heart the generosity to acknowledge that there is a small nation that has stood alone, not for one year or two, but for several hundred years against aggression . . . that was clubbed many times into insensibility, but that each time, on regaining

consciousness, took up the fight anew. A small nation that could never accept defeat and never surrender her soul.

John Hume epitomised the solid, respectable, church-going, conscientious working-class people of Derry. Eamonn McCann represented another social strand. McCann's father, like John Hume's, was a trade unionist. While Hume's father worked into the night, writing letters on behalf of people being denied welfare rights, McCann's father was a vocal advocate of socialism and institutional change. Their sons grew up in the same kind of two-up, two-down house. John and Eamonn both won scholarships to a grammar school. Both took advantage of the 1947 Education Act to go on to university. Eamonn was not, to put it mildly, attracted to the religious life, and chose to go Queen's University in Belfast.

Only the breadth of a Bogside street separated the McCanns' house from ours. Maureen, Eamonn's sister, was a regular visitor, but Eamonn's request to see me came as quite a surprise. He wanted information on the credit-union movement. Probably writing a thesis, I thought. We settled down on either side of the fire in the sitting room. I was in my element, describing the humble beginnings of the movement in Germany in the last century, and its spread to Canada, the United States and the Caribbean. It had survived the Depression in the early 1930s and two world wars; in the late 1950s it arrived in Ireland. McCann listened intently, occasionally nodding his mop of curly hair or asking a short, clipped question. He seemed to be comparing credit unionism with his own vision of a united working-class movement. I wound up with a summary of the success of the local credit union. I described how it had brought people together to solve their own problems, and gave Eamonn an idea of our membership and told him of the funds which could be invested in the community. In particular I dwelt on the new feeling of confidence among many of the members. I made the case that change could be brought about when people became involved in solving their own problems. The young Eamonn McCann was not impressed. Rising abruptly to his feet, he said, 'You are only papering over the cracks in this society', and left.

I was stung by his curt remark. For more than an hour I sat there, evaluating my own contribution to the community over the years. I had worked for youth clubs, charities and the credit union. I had an impeccable track record. I was also holding down a senior position in a Protestant construction company, an unheard-of achievement for a Catholic Bogsider. The house I was sitting in I had built with my own hands. I was struggling to pay off a mortgage and bring up a large family. What more could be expected from me? McCann was being educated at the taxpayer's expense. As far as I knew he had never earned a penny in his life, yet he had spurned my values. At first I was angry with him, and with myself. I had allowed him to needle me and expose the smugness of my position. I took pride in coming up with solutions for the problems of Northern Ireland, and now McCann was accusing me of being part of the problem.

His vision of working-class unity ran contrary to my experience of the realities of life in Derry. How far apart Catholics and Protestants really were became clear to me during the funeral of John Eakin, the founder of the company for which I worked. Even at the age of ninety-five, John Eakin had been active and alert. He seemed to have a fair chance of making it to the age of one hundred. But that was not to be. The old man fell one day, and sustained a severe and untreatable wound to the back of his head. He died as a result of a simple accident, instead of slipping out of life in the comfort of his bed. The company closed on the day of his burial. All of the workers attended his funeral. The service was held in a red-brick church at the top of the Rock Road; afterwards he was buried in the city cemetery.

Eakin's had a mixed workforce. The Protestants filed into the church, while the Catholics stood outside, stamping their feet in the light covering of snow that had fallen during the night. For them to enter the building would have been to recognise that those who had left the Church during the Reformation had had some right on their side. As the funeral cortège slowly made its way to the cemetery, the Christians mixed once again, only to separate once more when they arrived at the open grave. I watched Danny McLaughlin, a gentle giant of a man from Inishowen who had served the company for many years, help carry the oak casket from the carriage to the grave. The Catholic McLaughlin stood beside the white-surpliced Protestant minister as he intoned the prayers before the interment. Taking courage from McLaughlin's presence at the graveside, I left my workmates and stepped across the few yards of earth which divided the two groups, separating Protestant prayers from Catholic ears. I was careful not to mingle, and remained on the fringe. We might all come together, Catholics and Protestants, at occasions such as funerals, but there was no prospect of political consensus. Eamonn McCann's united working class was light years away. Protestant workers had no intention of entering into any kind of pact with their Catholic counterparts. Most of them backed a political system which conferred economic advantages on them, its supporters.

James Hegarty, leader of the Nationalist Party in Londonderry Corporation, bore within himself the accumulated frustrations of the nationalist community. In the council chamber, time out of number he had tried to interest Unionist politicians in the plight of his community; he always failed. Arrogant in their corrupt possession of power, the Unionist Party ignored the Nationalist Party and the people it spoke for. The nationalist population, 70 per cent of the whole, had only eight representatives on the corporation while the unionist population, 30 per cent of the whole, had twelve members. The Unionist Party showed only contempt for the opposition: they refused to debate any political, social or economic issue seriously. Their tactics were crude but effective. The Unionist councillors proposed and seconded any motion they wished to pass. Without bothering to debate the motion with their opponents, they simply used their majority to carry it. On the other hand, a motion from a member of the Nationalist Party would encounter a stony silence and inevitably be defeated on a show of hands. Hegarty memorably expressed his frustration after one of these sectarian votes. Looking towards the opposition benches he said, 'For God's sake, will some of you speak? I have been here eleven years and I have never heard the sound of your voices. I only know the colour of your hands as they are raised against us.' The disenfranchised and homeless Catholics admired Hegarty's eloquence and energy, although he could do little to help them.

High-rise flats seemed to offer new hope for homeless families in cities where building land was scarce. Architects and planners changed the face of Europe during the building boom of the 1950s and 1960s, convincing politicians that the benefits of stacking families on top of each other far outweighed the disadvantages. The concept was floated in Derry and bought by the politicians there, although there was no scarcity of land in the city. With a population of about 65,000, Derry was little more than a large country town with an agricultural hinterland. So desperate was the housing shortage in Catholic areas that the Nationalist Party quickly agreed to the housing of the homeless in high-rise flats. Its leaders may even have considered this an important breakthrough in a town which had the worst public-housing record in Western Europe. But political considerations lay behind what seemed to be a humanitarian gesture on the part of our rulers.

In the 1920s the government of Northern Ireland adjusted the boundaries of the electoral wards within Derry in order to give a unionist minority permanent control of a predominantly nationalist city. Since then the unionist rulers had carefully monitored and adjusted electoral boundaries in the city. The gerrymander divided Derry into three electoral wards. The north and Waterside wards had unionist majorities and populations of 6,500 and 5,500 respectively in 1966. The two wards regularly returned twelve Unionist councillors between them. The south ward was almost entirely nationalist, with a voting population of approximately 11,000, and regularly returned eight Nationalist councillors. As long as this arrangement persisted, the nationalist population would have no influence on political life in the city.

The proposed flats reflected some neat sectarian thinking: by building them, the corporation could claim to be doing something to ease overcrowding; by locating them in the Bogside, in the centre of the nationalist bantustan, it ensured that the political balance on the corporation would remain undisturbed. In the mid-1960s, Nationalist councillors – many of whose electors were living in overcrowded accommodation – went along with the corporation's plans. At the time, I didn't give much thought to the scheme. Brick, concrete, timber and steel were my life. I had seldom thought about the social implications of the work I loved. I was as hard as the materials with which I worked and which in turn shaped me. To build well, quickly and cheaply meant more to me than any religion. I had another agenda: in my work I pushed myself to the limit in order to prove that a Catholic was as capable as any Protestant.

Eileen was the first to foresee the social problems high-rise flats would bring, and upbraided me for my lack of interest in them. At her insistence I went to see a neighbour of ours, Jack Boyce. Jack had already spoken out against the new building complex, and was in the process of constructing a scale model of the proposed fourteen-storey building towering over the adjacent housing. Once finished, the model went on public display: we put it in a trailer, hitched the trailer to a car and toured the area. After our 'publicity drive', we arranged a meeting with Councillor James Doherty, the chairman of the Nationalist Party and an elected member of the corporation. Doherty was insistent. Catholics were in desperate need of housing. The Unionist politicians would not permit houses to be built outside the south ward, so the flats would have to go up inside the south ward. If that meant multi-storey accommodation, so be it. His attitude angered me. 'You are addressing the wrong problem and compounding the difficulties of the people. You would be better employed in trying to break the political stranglehold which keeps our people in subjection instead of settling for short-term solutions,' I bawled at him. This exchange reinforced my conviction that the Nationalist leadership was no longer effective. It had no power or direction. It would have to go before any real progress could be made.

Jim McGreneragh and I made a presentation to Londonderry Corporation on behalf of those who opposed the building of the fourteen-storey high-rise apartment block. Knowing that we had no chance of support from the Nationalist Party, we made a pitch to the Unionist councillors and aldermen. As the eight Nationalist votes would be cast in favour of the project, it was vital that we persuaded the Unionists to vote against something which they had already decided to accept. We based our presentation on good old-fashioned Protestant precepts: hard work; taking responsibility for the well-being of one's family and community; investing money and effort for future reward. I studied the faces of our listeners and reckoned we were making a good impression. Councillor Doherty, Chairman of the Nationalist Party, certainly thought so. As he left the council chamber he whispered to me, with grudging admiration: 'You are a cunning bastard.'

'When I fight, I fight to win,' I replied.

CHAPTER 4

I was never officially informed that our protest had been successful. But when building work began, I noticed that the original design had changed; the finished complex of houses and maisonettes would look much better than I had expected. My friends and I had successfully opposed the original fourteen-storey block of flats, but the design alterations represented a placatory gesture rather than a change of policy. Political, rather than humanitarian considerations lay behind the development.

If the system of gerrymandering (imported from America) had not existed, the unionists would have invented it. Having controlled political life, trade and commerce in the city for more than three and a half centuries, they now believed they owned the place. Their hold on the city was obsessive; their unwillingness to share it with the rest of its citizens strangled its development. The walled city, which the unionists proudly called 'the Maiden City' – because it had never been taken in a siege – was like a kept woman: possessed but not really loved by her master. She was hated by the Catholics, who had never been allowed to appreciate her charm.

The first complex of flats was built on the site of the old Rossville Street Market. As this is boggy land, the builders had to drive piles down to the bedrock. Little did I realise, as I saw the concrete-framed structure take shape, that it would, in turn, help shape the political future of Northern Ireland. The Bogside flats were built under the shadow of the monument to Governor Walker, who directed the defence of the city during the siege of 1689. This assault lasted for 114 bloody days. The citizens of Derry starved and died to mount an act of rebellion against their rightful monarch, King James II. On the base of the monument are engraved the names of the thirteen apprentices who shut the gates of the city against King James's army. The governor, carved in stone, stood atop a fluted column about a hundred feet high, his forefinger pointing northward to Culmore, where a ship, the *Mountjoy*, broke the wooden boom across the Foyle and relieved the besieged city.

We usually ignored this triumphalist symbol, save on those occasions when Orangemen and Apprentice Boys converged on Derry from all parts of Ireland, and further afield, to commemorate Governor Walker. Like pilgrims on the road to a holy site, they beat their drums and flew their flags, marching and proclaiming their belief in God and God's belief in them.

Nationalists approached every poll with a sense of expectation. It was hard to understand why, because no election since the creation of the state had changed the political or social conditions under which most nationalists lived. Since Eddie McAteer's election in 1953, his only serious challenger had been Stephen McGonagle, a Labour candidate. But both Catholic and Protestant electors had given him the thumbs-down. Organised opposition to the Nationalist Party in the Catholic ghettos in Derry had since collapsed. All the same, when an election was announced in 1965, we felt that the people would welcome a new approach to politics. We sensed that the Nationalist Party was becoming unsure of itself, and that it was losing hope of ever effecting change. Since McGonagle, only one other person with the potential for creative leadership had surfaced: John Hume.

A meeting took place in my house. It was attended by John Hume, Michael Canavan, John Bradley JP, Dr Jim Cosgrove, Pat Deeney and a few others. Starting around 8pm, we explored the need for a new political strategy and discussed the state of the Nationalist Party and the possibility of Hume winning the election. Canavan was sure that a frontal attack on the Nationalist

Party was the way to go about it, but Hume was unwilling to take the risk. He cast considerable doubt on the ability of those present to mount a campaign strong enough to get him elected. After a frustrating six-hour debate, with Hume stonewalling, never saying yes and never saying no, Dr Jim Cosgrove lost his temper and attacked John for his faint-heartedness: 'I thought you had the ability to give a lead to the people, but I was mistaken. You are looking for cast-iron guarantees which can't be given. We are looking for a leader, and you have shown you are not the man.' His face white with anger, he left the meeting. Its high hopes dashed and its energy dissipated, the caucus collapsed. Hume had obviously decided that a possible fall at the first hurdle was not the way to begin a political career.

Despite his previous disappointment with John Hume, Michael Canavan still believed that Hume had more capacity for leadership than anyone else in the north-west. Hume's ambivalence, when offered the opportunity to fight the Nationalist Party, reflected the fact that, in order to run for Parliament, he would have to give up his job as a teacher. Under Northern Irish legislation, teachers were barred from standing for election to Parliament. He wouldn't risk giving up his job unless he was guaranteed a seat. In a straight fight with McAteer, he might well have lost. Canavan later resolved the difficulty for Hume by opening a small salmon-curing business and employing Hume as its manager. He was grooming Hume for leadership and was backing his judgement with his own money. In the meantime, Hume took soundings and concluded that many grass-roots members of the Nationalist Party favoured a new approach to the political and economic problems besetting the nationalist community. He flirted with, and eventually joined, the Nationalist Party in order to seek the nomination in the event of McAteer standing down. 'If you can't beat them, join them,' I thought. McAteer also recognised Hume's potential, but wasn't ready to retire yet. Hume hadn't really proved himself politically, but his star was rapidly rising. There was a vague agreement that Eddie McAteer would stand down after one more term and hand over the reins to Hume, who by that time would have gained experience within the party. Other long-standing members would have to be considered, but the general feeling was that John Hume would eventually become leader of the Nationalist Party.

John now had two options. He could work within the structures of the Nationalist Party, in the expectation of assuming the mantle of leadership. This was his surest route to success at the polls. Alternatively, if his expectations were not realised, he could challenge any other nominee without losing his livelihood. While he was pondering the best way forward for him in his search for political power, the seeds of a great controversy were sown when the government decided to establish a second university in Northern Ireland.

New technology, cheap energy and an expanding world market had created an economic boom in Britain. The educational system was barely able to produce the numbers of skilled workers industry required. The British government decided to build more universities. Northern Ireland had one university, Queen's in Belfast, and a university college, Magee, in Derry. When it was announced that Northern Ireland was to have a second university, it didn't occur to anyone in Derry that it could be sited anywhere else but in their city. In size and importance, Derry was the second city of the north, and Magee College had a long association with university education. Anyone with an ounce of sense or foresight could see the advantages in the new university being established as far as possible from Belfast, and you couldn't get further away than Derry.

For very practical reasons, both Catholic and Protestant families wanted the university in Derry. They wanted to avoid the expense of sending their children to university in Belfast. Parents were unhappy about sending their children into what many considered an environment injurious to faith and morals. The university would have been a shot in the arm for the city. For every job it directly created, it would have created another indirectly. But above all, Derry would finally have been confirmed as the second city of Northern Ireland. It would be a university city – a seat of learning once again after a hiatus of nearly a thousand years.

Education, particularly third-level education, meant a great deal to working-class Catholics. Traditionally they had advanced themselves by joining the priesthood, or by becoming bookmakers or publicans. Then the 1947 Education Act, which opened up higher education to the working classes, created a whole range of other possibilities. Some Catholic families had taken advantage of the opportunities it offered, and the first professionals to benefit from that legislation, of which John Hume was one, were beginning to assert themselves. My first son, John, had just joined the Law Faculty at Queen's University, and it was clear that other members of the family would go there as well. Hundreds of Derry families shared our aspirations. When the announcement was made, Derry's Catholics and Protestants found a common cause for the first time in generations.

In their naivety, the people believed that the siting of the new university was not a political issue. A campaign was launched to have the university sited in Derry, and local politicians were given to understand that they would best serve the interests of the people by remaining on the sidelines. The fragile consensus on the issue of a university wouldn't have survived politicisation. In his impatience, John Hume almost forfeited the chance to lead the campaign. If it had been widely known that he was a member of the Nationalist Party, he would not have been acceptable to the Protestants. Luckily for him, his membership was not generally known; by withdrawing his membership the party helped him reaffirm the clean, apolitical image which he had been prepared to shed if it had proved necessary to do so. It was a lucky break for John.

We confidently awaited the outcome of the government's deliberations. It was some time before we realised that political considerations would dictate where the new university would eventually be sited, for these weighed heaviest with the Unionist politicians making the decision. Those who partitioned Ireland wanted the boundaries of the new northern statelet to enclose the maximum amount of territory which the UK could safely govern. The population of Northern Ireland was roughly two-thirds loyalist and one-third nationalist. But the west of the statelet had a nationalist majority and the Unionist rulers came to fear that a prosperous west would threaten the stability of Northern Ireland. After fifty years of gerrymandering and discrimination, the western part of Northern Ireland was much more disadvantaged than the loyalist east.

Having cut his ties to the Nationalist Party, Hume was without formal political attachments and was able to play a prominent role in the campaign, with Michael Canavan doing the legwork behind the scenes. After a series of meetings, the leaders of the campaign decided to go to Stormont to put Derry's case to the government. A cavalcade of cars, their horns blaring, let the whole of Northern Ireland know that Derry was demanding to become a centre of learning once again. The campaign united Protestants and Catholics: the mayor, elected representatives and prominent citizens took the petition to the steps of Stormont. After it was delivered, I watched the mayor, Commander Anderson, address the large crowd outside parliament buildings. 'We have taken our case to the very steps of Parliament. We can do no more,' he told us.

To our enormous disappointment, the University of Derry campaign failed, but it would prove to be a watershed in modern

Irish history. The revelations that some of those who had led the cavalcade had already intimated to the government that a university in Derry would become nationalist-oriented and should be sited elsewhere, where the people's loyalty to the Northern Ireland government was beyond question, stunned us. Apparently, there was more than one Judas in Derry. It was suspected – and never denied – that a group of prominent Unionist businessmen who pretended they were supporting Derry's cause had secretly sold out the people. When the betrayal became public, the Unionist mayor denied all knowledge of the conspiracy; it was generally accepted that he had also been hoodwinked. Despite its failure, the campaign had primed the pump of political agitation and exposed the crude and cruel machinations of the Unionist Party. It had also catapulted John Hume into a new sphere of political activity.

My own hopes that Hume would provide the idealistic and radical leadership desperately needed by the nationalist population in Northern Ireland had been fading for some time, and his latest manoeuvre did nothing to restore them. For years we had been discussing politics together. We agreed that the Nationalist Party had become a buffer between the people and the government. Instead of helping the people to improve themselves, it was standing in the way of real progress. I knew all the Nationalist politicians, and without exception I admired them for their dedication and efforts on behalf of the Catholic people, but collectively, as an organisation, they only frustrated any genuine efforts at change. Hume and I had agreed that the Nationalist Party would have to be destroyed. Yet he had been prepared to join it for whatever advantage it could provide. My understanding of the political process was an instinctive one; my intellect and my instincts were perpetually at variance. My intellect told me that John was the best leader available, but deep down, I believed that he would go the way of all the previous leaders.

By 1967 the credit-union movement in Derry was an unqualified success, but our dreams of building houses, creating jobs, starting cooperatives and giving people power had given way to the day-to-day challenge of running Derry Credit Union. The weekly induction of new members, the regular meetings of committees, the collection of money and a host of other chores were absorbing the energy of people who, seven years before, had set out to change the face of Northern Ireland. We were now running a banking institution. There is no doubt that we were running it well. Membership was rapidly expanding, work had started on our new headquarters building and we enjoyed great prestige in the whole of Ireland. At chapter meetings in Northern Ireland, our representatives wielded tremendous influence. They commanded attention at the AGM of the Irish Credit Union League, which had been set up to strengthen and service the movement. When we spoke, either from the platform or from the floor in Dublin, Cork or Waterford, people listened. When we gave a lead, others followed. John Hume was a world vice-president, and I was president of the Derry Credit Union. We had helped initiate the greatest popular movement in modern Ireland. We were basking in the sunshine of our success.

CHAPTER 5

The O'Doherty clan was a sub-sept of the mighty O'Donnells, who were descended from Conn of the Hundred Battles. The tall, dark man who was courting Doreen, my first-born, bore the proud name of O'Donnell. I had mixed feelings when Eileen quietly told me that the marriage would take place in August that year. Her knitting needles flicked up and down as a new christening shawl for our thirteenth child took shape. I pretended to study the intricately patterned shawl that tumbled over her knees and onto the floor, while struggling with my conflicting emotions.

'Well, whatever will be, will be,' I replied finally.

The flicking stopped; there was a slight tone of annoyance in Eileen's voice. 'But my baby is also due in August!'

That night I discussed the proposed wedding arrangements with my daughter and suggested that the ceremony be postponed until after the birth. An alternative was to have it as soon as possible, to avoid a clash of events. Twelve hours later, we had decided to have the wedding at Easter, a time associated with new beginnings. As far as I knew, it was the first time a wedding had been brought forward because the bride's mother was pregnant.

We held the wedding reception in John F. McLaughlin's hotel in Malin – the 'tidiest town' in Ireland, in the north of the Inishowen peninsula. The guests included many of the new crop of educated Catholics. The only Protestant there was Ivan Cooper, a Labour activist, who would figure prominently in events to come. Michael Canavan took time out from the celebrations to ask me what was happening on the ground. I told him that the agitation on the streets by a few desperate people in need of houses and jobs would lead to a general mobilisation of the Catholic population. I was beginning to question my own efforts to get people to lift themselves up by their bootstraps; I was coming to believe that institutional change was an absolute necessity. I argued this point with Michael, who reiterated that the purpose of organisations like the credit union was to give people a sense of their own identity; to help them take control of their own financial affairs; and afford them opportunities for leadership.

As I turned to watch my daughter take the floor with her husband, Frank O'Donnell, in the first dance, I remembered the circumstances of her birth twenty years before, and my early struggle to provide a home. Eileen and I had begun our married life in one small room on the Strand Road, but when her pregnancy became noticeable, the landlord asked us to leave. We both went to live with my mother in the family home under Derry's walls. Before the birth, Eileen returned to her mother's house, as expectant mothers often did at the time. A few weeks after Doreen was born she returned, and shortly afterwards we found two rooms on the second floor of a house on Carlisle Road. One year and three months later, our second child, John L. was born. At twenty-three years of age, I was feeling the strain of living in deplorable conditions while trying to hold down a job. Our two children were confined to a second-floor two-roomed apartment fronting onto a main thoroughfare, on the eastern side of the old city. One external toilet served three families and a ground-floor tap and sink were the only sources of water. Occasionally, the news that a Catholic had got a house in the new Creggan Estate, which overlooked the Bogside, would raise our hopes. One day I decided to take time off work to go to the Housing Office of Londonderry Corporation. The corporation was legally obliged to build houses for its unemployed and low-waged citizens. After a lengthy wait, the housing manager appeared at the counter in the office. After listening to my enquiry he looked over his reading glasses and asked me how many children I had.

'Two,' I replied.

With a gesture of annoyance, he snapped, 'Come back in nine years and I'll take your name.'

I swore under my breath in despair. Hatred of Unionist politicians, who had the city by the throat, welled up within me.

Michael interrupted my reminiscences. He pursued his argument, warning me that there was too much at stake, and that any involvement in street agitation might damage the credit-union movement, which he believed needed a little more time to establish itself. I was still adamant about the need for direct action. He asked me to wait until the end of the year, when both of us could resign from our respective credit unions (Canavan was president of Pennyburn Credit Union and I was president of Derry Credit Union) and go onto the streets together.

The Unionists discriminated, gerrymandered, and denied people their right to vote, in order to keep themselves in power. These were the more obvious aspects of their oppressive rule. By far the most sinister was the infamous Civil Authorities (Special Powers) Act, which became law in April 1922, before Northern Ireland was even a year old. The act was so manifestly ugly and repressive that those who had drawn it up promised to destroy it after a year. But it served its purposes so well that it was reprieved every year until 1928. By then, the government had become so attached to its misshapen monster that it granted it another five years of life. In 1933 the act was made permanent. Under its terms, the Minister of Home Affairs became the civil authority in Northern Ireland. He had the power to take all steps and issue all orders necessary for preserving peace and maintaining order. The act also gave him the power to extend his authority to matters not specifically provided for in the act. Seldom has so much power been placed in the hands of one man. He could suspend trial by jury, imprison without trial, have prisoners whipped and refuse to hold inquests. The minister had the power to restrict or ban the holding of meetings or processions; to forbid the ownership or use of a motor vehicle by any person; to destroy private buildings or property for the purpose of the act; to prohibit the circulation of newspapers and the staging and screening of plays and films. He could delegate to ordinary policemen the authority invested in himself, and the same policemen had the power to arrest anyone they suspected of entertaining criminal thoughts. There were years, during the period from 1922 to 1968, when the level of crime was so low that the government began closing police stations. One would have thought that in these circumstances, good sense would have suggested the abolition of the Special Powers Act. But good sense was always a rare commodity in the North. Policemen and B-Specials carried on spying on Catholics as a means of creating a purpose for their own armed existence.

The B-Specials were a part-time, exclusively Protestant paramilitary force who paraded and trained with their .303 rifles, treating everyone to displays of their arrogance. Although they all had full-time jobs, they would counter moves to downsize the force during periods of peace by creating an illusory war, shooting at anything that moved in the darkness of the countryside; now and then a cow would meet an untimely death at their hands. Every week the 'B-men' would strip and clean weapons in their homes throughout Northern Ireland, reinforcing the myth that Protestants were a community under siege. They still believed they were defending civil and religious liberties won during the Reformation and defended successfully in 1689 and 1690, at Derry, Enniskillen and the Boyne.

The struggle for civil liberties in Derry in the 1960s was led by Bridget Bond, who was married to an Englishman and the mother of a large family. The essential difference between me and my 'up-by-our-own-bootstraps' brigade and Bridget Bond was that we had houses and jobs and were registered voters. Bridget needed change because she had neither a house nor a job and was disenfranchised. Bridget's lonely struggle came to an end when Eamonn McCann and Eamonn Melaugh and others brought the politics of direct action to Derry, in March 1968. Their Derry Housing Action Committee (DHAC) broke up a meeting of Londonderry Corporation, causing consternation among Nationalist as well as Unionist representatives. The RUC removed the DHAC protesters, who came back for more in April and May. On 22 June, the members of DHAC used a caravan to block a road. It was a fairly low-key protest, but it brought a reaction from the authorities. Within a month the Bond family had been rehoused. McCann and Melaugh were fined in court for obstructing traffic. I had a feeling that jail sentences would have suited their purposes better.

I took stock of the sudden proliferation of organisations that were making public statements and demonstrating. It was hard to distinguish one from another but McCann and Melaugh appeared to be pulling the strings. I couldn't make up my mind whether they were motivated by concern for the underprivileged or were simply trying to create as much chaos as possible. The unconstitutional actions of the DHAC came as a shock to the Catholics of Derry. The DHAC activists caused indignation in the Nationalist Party and embarrassment throughout a community steeped in the traditions of forbearance and respect for authority. It was one thing to complain against discrimination, but it was quite another to do something about it, especially if such action meant breaking the law. They might be poor, homeless, jobless and second-class, but they were law-abiding, respectable people, unused to raising their voices in public. They had politicians to do that for them. Catholics believed in representative democracy and leadership from above. They had been born into a system that did not encourage them to believe in their own power.

On 26 June 1968, in Caledon, County Tyrone, Austin Currie joined a protest against the allocation of a newly built house to a single Protestant woman in an area where many Catholic families were homeless. He illegally occupied the house and was removed by the police. Currie's action was as unlawful as any of McCann's but he lacked the pugnacity and stridency that characterised Derry Housing Action Committee. Austin Currie wasn't a radical seeking to overthrow the state, but his eviction by the police and the subsequent publicity did make housing a national issue.

The Unionists who controlled Londonderry Corporation displayed an incredible level of insensitivity. The mayor had the final say in the allocation of houses. At a time when people and the media were taking a keen interest in the corporation's housing policy, the mayor granted a house to a Protestant applicant from Belfast. Hundreds of local families were desperately waiting for housing; the greatest humiliating indignity would have been for them to lose out to a local Protestant, never mind one from seventy-five miles away, who had simply jumped the housing queue. Here was proof – if proof was needed – of the Unionists' disregard for the needs of Catholic families. James Hegarty, the leader of the Nationalist Party in Derry, demanded an explanation, but was ignored.

Power corrupts, but also blinkers those who wield it; they seem to grow oblivious to changing circumstances in the world around them. The Unionists had established their own power base, created a one-party state, written their own rule book, organised their own security forces and appointed their own judiciary; they now believed that their system would last forever. That a handful of activists demanding fair allocation of houses might threaten their power never occurred to them. When James

Hegarty made his protest in the Council Chambers, those same activists scoffed at him from the public gallery and accused him of jumping on their bandwagon. Eamonn McCann was succeeding beyond his wildest dreams, and he had every intention of keeping his hand on the tiller. The becalmed ship had been nudged by a wind of change.

Discounting the Nationalist Party, which appeared to be impotent, there were now two main political currents within nationalist Derry. The first was the 'bootstraps brigade': Canavan, Hume, myself, and several others from the credit-union movement, together with Father Mulvey and his Housing Association, and Niall McCafferty and a group of young teachers who were involved in job-creation. In the main, the leaders were the products of the 1947 Education Act. We posed a threat to no one, but were involved in good paternalistic activity. We were full of hope and had a tremendous capacity for good work. The second grouping, led by Eamonn McCann and Eamon Melaugh, advocated direct action. Its slogans were 'one man, one vote'; 'one man, one house' and 'one man, one job'. For the first time, in unequivocal language, people were spelling out their demands; some were prepared to go beyond the law to attain them. McCann had no respect for us, nor we for him. Hume said, 'I can go along with "one man, one vote" and "one man, one house", but "one man, one job" is revolution.'

But events would bring the two groupings together before the year was out. McCann and the direct action group organised a march for 21 July to commemorate the centenary of the birth of James Connolly. The march was banned, but a rally was held instead in a car park in Foyle Street. Gerry Fitt, the MP for West Belfast, wearing a white shirt, addressed the crowd. Fitt's survival in politics owed much to his acute understanding of working-class feelings; he was now tuning in to their mood, as he had done so often in the past. He rolled up his sleeves: 'There are people prepared to accept Terence O'Neill because he walks over you with bedroom slippers, while Paisley would walk over you with hobnailed boots. I am not prepared to let anyone walk over me, in any circumstances . . . '

In August, the Northern Ireland Civil Rights Association (NICRA) organised a march from Coalisland to Dungannon, to protest against discrimination in the allocation of housing in the Dungannon area. The march was well-attended and very peaceful, but the RUC made sure it never reached its destination. In a healthy society, the police would have facilitated such a peaceful protest, but Northern Ireland was far from healthy. The executive of NICRA sent a delegation to Derry to meet the group controlled by McCann and Melaugh; both sides agreed to hold a march in Derry on 5 October. The organisers later discovered, to their disappointment, that the date clashed with a Derry City home game at the Brandywell. The route chosen for the march was that traditionally taken by the Orangemen. The visiting delegates might not have been aware of this, but McCann's group was. They also succeeded in getting two members of NICRA to sign a document notifying the police of the route of the proposed march, as they were legally required to do. On Thursday 3 October, the Northern Ireland Minister of Home Affairs, William Craig, banned the march. NICRA called an urgent meeting in Derry. Would they or would they not defy the ban? Kevin Agnew, the Republican delegate on the executive, and a lawyer, declared, 'If the people of Derry are marching tomorrow, I am marching with them.' The Direct Action Group was doing well: after harnessing NICRA's energy and respectability in the pursuit of political chaos, they had received a gift from the Minister of Home Affairs.

Meanwhile, John Hume, assisted by an extremely capable board of directors in Derry, had shot to prominence in the international credit-union movement. He had a tremendous capacity for work and for travelling and meeting people, and had already burned out two Morris Minors. He travelled the length and breadth of Ireland, founding and assisting credit unions. He was now president of the Irish Credit Union League and a world vice-president of the movement. He had been invited to speak as a guest at the International Credit Union Day celebrations in Australia. He was very tempted to go. He would have circled the globe and called on various leaders of the movement en route. It would have been fitting recognition of his contribution to the credit-union movement and would have confirmed his stature in the movement. But Michael Canavan wasn't happy about John leaving Derry for any length of time: the smoking volcano was turning red around the rim. McCann and Melaugh may have been making the running, but Hume's popularity was soaring among the people. Under pressure from Michael, John turned down the invitation. The Irish credit-union movement was about to lose its best-known personality to politics.

I had taken to attending the occasional game at the Brandywell with Tommy Carlin, a fellow-director of Derry Credit Union, and had been looking forward to Saturday's match. But McCann and Melaugh were going ahead with their proposed march. Having made the mistake in their choice of date and ended up in competition with the football match, they went all-out to whip up support for the march. They put up posters and drove around the city with a loudspeaker. Most people paid no attention. But Craig's announcement of a ban on the march changed everything for me. I was unwilling to be sucked into McCann and Melaugh's scheme to cause disruption, but I was incensed by the minister's action. My ambivalence was shared by Carlin, but not by my son, John L. 'Craig's challenge is not only to the civil-rights movement, but to all of the Catholics in Derry, because he has identified them as the same people. He has to be confronted, or we will never get off our knees,' he declared. Shamed into making a stand, Carlin and I headed for the march with the young student.

We walked to the Waterside station, where we found about 200 people standing about in groups in the large, open area in front of the station. McCann, Melaugh and Ivan Cooper were much in evidence. Cooper was moving about from one group to another. I went up to him and shook his hand. In a short time, the crowd had doubled. Eddie McAteer and James Doherty joined the gathering as it came together under the direction of a handful of marshals wearing white arm bands. Gerry Fitt took up his position at the head of the march, accompanied by a group who were obviously strangers to Derry. People said that they were MPs from England. Television cameras were scanning the marchers and some interviews were taking place. Although there was no sign of the threatened loyalist counter-demonstration, people felt apprehensive. It wasn't the first time that many of those present had taken part in an illegal march, and they were all well aware that the organisers would, eventually, be charged with breaking the law. But the occasion lacked a sense of high drama. It was *Macbeth* with only two witches stirring the pot. Someone must have made the decision to organise things, because everyone gradually began drifting into the middle of the road. Over on the waste ground opposite the station, about twenty men were standing around watching us, perhaps trying to make up their minds whether to join the protest or not. People on the road were talking and not paying much attention to the marshals. Like horses in the Grand National, they milled around while the starter tried to get them into line. Word came through that Duke Street was blocked by the police. The tension was rising; suddenly we were away. John Hume left the waste ground and joined us just before the off.

It was difficult to understand why the marchers moved off so quickly. Almost at a trot they headed down into the hollow of Duke Street. Only when they met the rising ground at the southern end did the pace slacken.

Duke Street had seen better days: the buildings, three and four storeys high, slumped against each other. Shops, which had served a busy thoroughfare when Derry had four railway stations, were now scheduled for demolition to make way for a new approach road to Craigavon Bridge. Not for one moment did I think that a new politics was about to be hammered out on the anvil of civil rights. John L., Tommy Carlin and I were in the middle of the march when it came to a halt. There were shouts and the sounds of a scuffle. The makeshift placards demanding 'One Man, One Vote' obscured what was happening at the front, but it was obvious that the march had reached the end of the line. The missing witch, in the form of the RUC, had joined McCann and Melaugh in preparing the brew.

I didn't know anything about Betty Sinclair except that she was a member of the Communist Party. She began to speak, but I had no interest in what she had to say. The capitalist system was bad and there was ample evidence of its failure to serve the needs of people, but communism, for all its idealism, had proved in practice to be far more vicious, more repressive and less respectful of individual liberty. Fiercely individualistic, I had an ideal of a nation of people accepting responsibility for each other, in a country governed with the least possible intervention by the state. 'Let's scout around,' I said to Carlin. We moved to the back of the crowd. It was then that we saw the police, who had taken up positions behind us when the marchers had come to an enforced halt. They were stretched right across Duke Street, cutting off our escape. We were caught between a rock and a hard place.

There were other speakers after Betty Sinclair but I didn't listen to them either. The old buildings on either side of the street seemed to take on a new character. They were no longer decrepit and tired, but dark and solid, like the walls of a prison. I looked around for an open door or a space where we could shelter, but saw none. The rally grew noisier. I watched the rear line of policemen react by drawing their batons and crouching forward like runners in a race, poised and waiting for the starter's pistol. 'We don't have a chance if they charge us,' I said to Carlin. 'It's time to get offside.' About twenty yards of empty, open ground separated us from the line of policemen. We had a choice: we could rejoin the protesters, or head towards the police behind us before the fun started. With feigned nonchalance, Tommy and I walked the twenty yards towards the defenders of the statelet. Staring straight ahead, awaiting orders, the policemen scarcely noticed us as we eased our way through their ranks. We had just got through when a tremendous shout went up from the crowd at the other barricade. I turned and saw makeshift placards flying through the air and the policemen, like young bulls stung by picadors' darts, charging the marchers. I watched the police swing their batons, hitting heads, backs and shoulders. Private parts received short, vicious thrusts. Those still standing broke and ran. Carlin and I reached Fountain Hill ahead of the crowd. As we ran up the hill, Eamonn McCann shot by. I envied him his youth and lengthened my own stride to get as far away as possible from the police and back to the safety of the Bogside. I hoped that John L. had not been caught or injured by the RUC.

Tommy Carlin and I decided to double back along a parallel road, and arrived breathless at the approaches to Craigavon Bridge. The policemen hadn't bothered to follow the people they had missed in their first charge; instead they ploughed on through the crowd until they met their comrades coming the other way. Boots, fists, officers' blackthorn sticks and constables' truncheons took an unmerciful toll on the marchers. That day more than a hundred of them, including Gerry Fitt, were treated in Altnagelvin Hospital, mostly for head wounds. The RUC soon dealt with the weak resistance offered by some of the younger marchers, then they turned their attention to the people on the bridge. Water cannons were turned on everyone in sight and shoppers stood astounded as, with each pass, the water cannons plastered clothes against sodden bodies. Throughout this one-sided confrontation, the TV cameras rolled, recording the brutality and ineptitude of the RUC. I had never seen a water cannon in action before and it was the first time that people in Ireland or England had seen the RUC in action. No other police force in the civilised world would have boxed in the marchers as the RUC had in Derry. The first principle of peacekeeping is to allow a path of retreat for the protesters.

Quickly, Carlin and I made our way into the walled city. A large group had gathered in the Diamond, which features a memorial to the honoured dead of two world wars. It consists of a flat-chested, bronze-winged angel of victory on top of a pillar of sandstone, crushing the head of a snake with her foot. One of her hands holds aloft a laurel wreath, the other a naked sword. At a lower level stands a sailor straining against the wind, his trouser legs rolled up and his large, bronze toes dark green with age. On the other side, balancing the tableau, is a soldier, his flat, tin helmet tightly secured with a chinstrap, his rifle and bayonet raised to plunge into a fallen enemy. Four plaques crowded with the names of local men who gave their lives complete the memorial. It is a grotesque reminder of the horrors of war. Rumour had it that the monument had been built for a city in England, but the city fathers there had had second thoughts about it, so Londonderry Corporation bought it at half its original price. Few cities in the world could boast of having a second-hand war memorial.

The marchers regrouped around the monument. No longer surrounded by the police, they were noisily giving vent to their anger. A police car stopped in Shipquay Street. A sergeant and two constables got out. The sergeant remained by the car as the two constables walked towards the marchers. 'Out! Out! RUC! Out! Out! RUC!' chanted the crowd. The constables stood looking at us with contempt, and the shouts soon lost some of their venom. I felt confused. Respect for the law was part and parcel of a Catholic upbringing in Derry and it wasn't easy to go against the grain. Scanning the crowd, the policemen caught sight of a young man holding aloft a placard and moved swiftly towards him, pushing people aside. Seizing the defiant youth, they frogmarched him in the direction of the police car. He offered no resistance. The tension rose, as more policemen appeared on the fringe of the crowd. His feet barely touching the ground, each of his arms firmly held by a policeman, the slight youth was dragged up in front of the hefty-looking sergeant. He drove his fist deep into the young man's unprotected stomach. The youth slumped forward unconscious and was flung into the back of the waiting police car. The crowd erupted. That night Derry experienced its worst riots in nearly fifty years.

CHAPTER 6

The small houses of the Protestant enclave of Fountain Street weren't much different from the houses in the Bogside, and the conditions in which their inhabitants lived were only marginally better. The men may have been employed but they were usually in low-paid jobs. Their employers were not noted for their generous treatment of their workers but they did provide security of a sort for the Protestant working class. The Unionist Party used a subtle blend of paternalism, bribery and scare-mongering to keep the Protestant people in line; the doors of opportunity would be slammed in the faces of any hardy individuals who criticised or stepped outside the system. I remembered a story my father once told me about a group of striking Protestant workers. They were confronted by a manager holding a flag in each hand. 'Which will it be?' he asked. 'Will you join the rebels under this flag?' – he held up the green, white and orange tricolour – 'or will you remain loyal to this?' he asked, holding up the Union flag. The strike collapsed.

I recalled my father's story when Ivan Cooper called to my door seeking my support for the civil-rights movement. I admired Cooper – he was his own man – and was agreeably surprised that he had called. His red hair, lightened at the ends by the summer sun, surrounded his round, full face, giving him an almost cherubic appearance. But there was nothing angelic in his forceful way of making a play for my support. The differences between us surfaced when Cooper described his fight for change *within* Northern Ireland. Unlike him, I wanted an end to Northern Ireland.

'I love the constitution of this country. I love its flag and all it stands for. I am a loyal Protestant who is seeking civil rights for all the people of the country, Catholic as well as Protestant,' he declared.

I had nothing but respect for the young civil-rights leader, but I couldn't go along with his thinking: 'This state was set up by force of arms against the wishes of the majority of the Irish people, and it has been maintained by coercion and corruption. The civil rights you talk about have been denied Catholics so that they would always remain a powerless minority. They have been refused votes, houses and jobs, to drive them from this country, in order to perpetuate a Protestant parliament for a Protestant people. The march yesterday has awakened the sleeping giant of Irish nationalism and the last phase of the journey towards freedom from the domination of England has begun.'

My own frank, undiluted nationalism shocked Cooper, who shot back, 'You are nothing but a Catholic bigot.'

'If seeking the unity of this country means I am a bigot, then a bigot I am,' I retorted.

Craig congratulated the RUC on its handling of the protest. The brutality his force had displayed shocked television viewers around the world. Anticipating more violence, hordes of reporters arrived in Derry. Their presence made another confrontation all the more likely. Eamonn McCann and his group were preparing for another attempt to march from Duke Street to the city centre. Cooper had offered me a chance to get involved in the struggle for civil rights. I had declined it because the labour movement, to which he and many of those engaged in the agitation belonged, had traditionally supported the Union, and I hated the Union with a passion. But I sympathised with the campaign for civil rights and was feeling annoyed at myself for having quarrelled with him. I was relieved to receive an invitation from James Doherty to attend a meeting in the City Hotel, to discuss the crisis facing Derry.

Wednesday 9 October came round. It was obvious that someone had formally booked the large room of the City Hotel, which was now filled to capacity, but no one appeared to know who that someone was. Neither McCann nor Melaugh had booked the room or called the meeting. They were angry at what they considered to be an attempt to hijack the movement which they had laboriously built up over a period of months. McCann took the chair. In a defiant tone he outlined the roles of the various organisations involved in the agitation preceding Saturday's march. He repeated his intention of maintaining his group's independence. He was supported by many of his confrères, who were annoyed by what they saw as interference from 'Johnnies-come-lately.'

Their anger abated when previously uncommitted people pledged to work for change. The large room, now packed to capacity, throbbed with energy and emotion as speaker after speaker condemned the government and the brutality displayed by the RUC and praised the courage of the organisers of the march. The resentment which had built up over fifty helpless years found expression in militant demands for immediate action; these alternated with calls for caution and planning. As the meeting progressed, the activists came under pressure from the 'tacticians', and the mood began to shift towards a gradualist approach. Eamonn McCann could feel the leadership slipping from his grasp as his supporters began accepting the arguments being presented by the newly converted. The lack of structure and firm organisation in the splinter groups proved to be the undoing of his leadership. Initially these loose alignments, and the freedom and flexibility they offered, had attracted people. But they were not structured enough to survive a crisis. Structures were what we needed right now.

We set about establishing and electing a representative group to cooperate with the original organisers to form a Citizens'

Action Committee. McCann's objections were ignored, as eleven people were selected from the body of the hall. Eamonn angrily left the meeting, denouncing those elected, as 'middle-aged, middle-class and middle-of-the-road.' Four of his most important supporters remained in the room and were absorbed into the new group.

The vast majority of those present were Catholic and their first choice as leader of the new group would have been John Hume, had he played a part in the agitation. Instead we elected as chairman the flamboyant Protestant labourite, Ivan Cooper, demonstrating that we were above sectarianism. Two other Protestants were elected: Campbell Austin, who was from an established business family and Claude Wilton, a solicitor. The first action taken by the committee was to abandon plans to have a march the following Saturday along the banned route. The tension eased after this decision was made. Derry had been saved from disaster. There was general relief that control of the campaign for civil rights had passed from Eamonn McCann and his followers to the more solid, representative leaders of Citizens' Action.

After it had worked out a shopping list of demands, the first task for the new Citizens' Action Committee was to test public opinion. A sit-down protest was called for Saturday 19 October, in the Guildhall Square. But, had the newly elected committee not clearly and forthrightly reasserted the right of all citizens to march along the banned route in the very near future, the new alliance of nationalists, republicans, radicals, conservatives and workers would never have endured. Each and every one of the speakers solemnly promised to defy any restrictions the government placed on the people's right to march in any part of the city. The countdown, started by Eamonn McCann and his friends on 5 October, had stopped during the meeting on 9 October, and started again at the end of the evening. The committee agreed to report back to a public meeting in six weeks' time. Next day Campbell Austin, the liberal Protestant, stated that he could not condone or be associated with such an unlawful act as sitting down and blocking the traffic, and he resigned. I had a feeling that he had come under pressure from the establishment in the city and had used the sit-down protest as an excuse to leave.

The square, between the large, red sandstone Guildhall and the dark stones of the city walls, had been the scene of meetings and celebrations of many kinds over the years. But never before 19 October 1968 had 5,000 citizens sat in protest on the cold, hard ground under the black muzzles of the cannons poking through the battlements. Rain added to our discomfort but newspapers spread on the ground protected our clothes and fundaments from the worst of the wet and cold. The worshipful companies of London, who had supplied the cannons for the defence of the city and who in the past had pleaded the city's case to the English government, would have been impressed at the standards of decency, respectability and good conduct displayed by the citizens of the city they had founded 360 years before. The speeches were a mixture of respectable, indignant calls for civil rights and appeals for solidarity among the people of the city. Claude Wilton summed up the temper of the meeting with the words, 'Let us, both Catholics and Protestants, work together for the benefit of all the people.' Once the meeting was over, everyone gathered up the damp, crumpled newspapers and removed them from the square, leaving it as they had found it. I went up onto the walls and looked down. Not a scrap of evidence of our protest remained.

A gesture of generosity from the government at this point would have stopped the civil-rights campaign in its tracks. But generosity had never been part of the make-up of those who wielded power in Northern Ireland. A movement had been born on 5 October and endured a rain of police blows, but it had won the first round. By sitting peacefully on the wet ground, the citizens of Derry won the second round on 19 October. Both contestants then retired to their respective corners to prepare for the next round. The City Hotel became the headquarters of the Citizens' Action Committee. If its members were not in a plenary session, they were to be seen at the bar, in the lounge or in the lobby. Newspapermen, hungry for news, circulated freely. The atmosphere was electric and expectant. The time-out between rounds two and three lasted until 2 November. The government had offered no conciliatory gesture, so we marched along the banned route. Citizens were asked to line the pavements and the new leaders of the civil-rights campaign took to the streets for the first time. Spread out in three lines, they walked solemnly over what had now become one of the most famous stretches of road in Ireland. The exercise smacked of brinkmanship, but it worked. The policemen, careful to protect what was left of their good image, even removed some loyalist protesters who had blocked the Ferryquay Gate, one of the entrances to the walled city. As the members of the Citizens' Action Committee entered through the gateway, their supporters flooded the roadway behind them and swept through the city to the Guildhall. The meeting was enthusiastic but orderly. Round three to the people.

French news reporters, who were searching for similarities between the student unrest in their own country and the drama unfolding in Northern Ireland, quickly latched onto John Hume, who had an excellent command of French. The French media came to lionise him. As Terence O'Neill, the Prime Minister, was also fluent in French, the possibility of a debate on French television soon became a reality. John headed to Paris and, from the French capital, faced O'Neill; the latter had to forgo the trip because of a heavy workload and spoke instead from Stormont.

Few people in Northern Ireland were aware of the substance of their debate, but the idea of an Irish Catholic conversing comfortably in French on television must have troubled many unionists. I was proud of Hume; his polished performance reinforced my belief that Catholics would not be second-class citizens for much longer, and that the myth of the intellectual supremacy of the Protestant ruling class had been debunked.

Vincent Hanna, one of the labour lawyers advising the Derry Citizens' Action Committee, came under pressure on the night of 15 November. He had been advocating a silent eyeball-to-eyeball confrontation with the RUC across the police barricade on the following day. Any kind of verbal abuse or physical contact had to be avoided, and the principle of non-violence had to govern the encounter, at all costs. It wasn't easy for the left-wingers and Republican elements of the committee to accept the dictates of their advisers. These instructions included taking physical abuse from the police without retaliating. I didn't much agree with them either, although I was now responsible for implementing the committee's decisions, the Chief Marshal, Paul Grace having withdrawn to concentrate on his union work. The fear that the government would order their arrest and then ban the demonstration was uppermost in the minds of the members. We decided to suspend the final plans for the demonstration until the following morning. We arranged emergency procedures in case of police intervention, and each member was instructed to appoint and brief a deputy to take his place in the event of his arrest. For security reasons we decided not to meet at our normal venue, the City Hotel: instead, committee and deputies were to meet the following morning at eleven o'clock in Brendan Duddy's restaurant in William Street. Whoever was available then would constitute the organising committee for the demonstration and make the final arrange-· ments. The meeting then closed, to allow members time to contact and appoint their deputies and to attend services for peace in the Protestant and Catholic cathedrals.

Although ten years separated us, Donal McCafferty and I were very close friends. He had taught me to box and had corresponded with me when I had gone to England to work. Births, deaths and marriages had drawn us closer together; joys and sorrows shared had strengthened the bond. Donal had done sterling work as a civil-rights steward and it was only natural that I should turn to my very good friend when I had to choose a deputy for the march on 16 November. But it wasn't friendship alone which took me to the McCaffertys' house that night. The McCaffertys were one of the prominent Catholic families in Derry. Their service to the Church in the field of music was legendary.

Donal was manager of a chain store inside the old city. I had never seen him dressed in anything other than a very good suit, collar and tie. A man above reproach, he had exactly the image the civil-rights movement had established for itself in Derry, and one which I was anxious to maintain. I pushed the door, to discover McCafferty kneeling on the living-room floor with a collection of tools around him. He was hammering an aluminium pot lid, shaping it to fit inside the flat top of an American-style hunting cap. It took me a while to work out why McCafferty was making a crash helmet for himself. I watched, fascinated, as he got to his feet. Tucking a one-inch-thick circle of foam on top of the aluminium, he placed the cap on his head. 'What do you think of that?' he proudly asked. Without telling him why I had come over, I responded, 'It will certainly soften the weight of a policeman's baton.' Then Donal brought forth the rest of his defensive accoutrements and, like a knight of old preparing for battle, he ritually outfitted himself with shinguards, heavy boots and a heavy, short-belted overcoat with protective shoulder pads sewn into the lining. Thus attired, he paraded up and down the floor. Only his face, grim and determined as he thought of the morrow's mission, remained unprotected. After the events of 5 October, his was a sensible approach to the forthcoming protest. When he produced a heavy brass knuckleduster and a short rubber truncheon, I decided to go elsewhere for a deputy. Terry Doherty, a young schoolteacher agreed. Nothing expressed the frustration, fear and desperation felt by nationalists more than McCafferty's transformation from ultra-respectable citizen into expectant martyr. During heavy stoning of the civil-rights marchers by loyalists the following day, McCafferty was injured. He was trying to restrain the younger marchers, standing with arms outstretched in a Christ-crucified pose, when he was struck in the face – the only unprotected part of his body – by a rock. He could not understand his friends' black jokes as they watched the blood from his lacerated mouth flow freely onto his heavily protected overcoat.

Catholics were invited to come to St Columb's Cathedral to pray for peace. It was the first time many of them had entered the cathedral, the first built by Protestants in Ireland after the Reformation. It must have contained a proud congregation at the first service in 1633. No second-hand Popish churches for the citizens of Londonderry. Like mourners filing past a funeral bier, people entered the cathedral in single file, processing past the hollowed-out cannon ball on its pedestal by the entrance. This had carried the terms of surrender dictated by the forces of King James II during the siege. The defenders of Derry returned it with a proud message: 'No Surrender!'

The hesitant movement they performed – something between a bow and a genuflection – identified the Catholics as they approached the high altar. They had come in their hundreds to pray for peace with their fellow Christians. We sought God's help: the immovable object – law and order – would meet the irresistible force of the civil-rights movement the following day, on the bridge which joined the Isle of Derry to the ancient parish of Glendermott. My eyes travelled along the Commonwealth flags proudly hanging on each side of the main aisle, and came to rest above the high altar on the two French standards which were captured by the defenders of Londonderry at the Battle of the Windmill in 1689. They had pride of place and evoked the defenders' gallant and rebellious struggle for civil and religious liberty against an English monarch. The silent organ pipes were surrounded by cherubim and seraphim, carved out of mahogany salvaged from a warship of the Spanish Armada that foundered on the rocks off Inishowen in September 1588.

That night sleep didn't come easily to me; I was uneasy about the lack of planning for the protest. I got up at dawn and prepared myself for the day ahead. Washed, shaved and fed, I headed for Michael Canavan's house, arriving just before nine o'clock. The place was already a hive of activity. Three of the young Canavans were scrubbing the Morris Mini which was to carry the public address system for the gathering that day. A blanket of suds covered the tiny car and a light breeze scattered wisps of foam across the lawn. Eileen Canavan put on the kettle while Michael and I discussed the difficulty of my role as chief marshal. I was not getting clear instructions. I expressed my displeasure: 'The committee has refused to appreciate the possibility of serious trouble today and is living in pious hope that it won't happen. My stewards are demanding instructions, particularly about what they should do if confronted by the police.'

Michael replied: 'Your very clear directions from the committee are to keep the peace at all costs.' I retorted in exasperation: 'Keeping the peace is hardly consistent with defying the minister's ban. The people are more concerned about asserting their right to march through their own city than keeping the peace.'

Derry was the Mecca of Orangeism, hence the insistence that no march, or meeting of Catholics, could be held inside its 360-year-old walls.

I was aware of the psychological importance of breaching the walls in defiance of Craig. I said to Canavan: 'We must get into the heart of the old city if we are to maintain the respect of the people. If we don't, they will despise us and we will be no better than those who have gone before us, leading the people right up to the mouth of the cannon and then abandoning them.'

Michael was stung by my words and said: 'The mandate of the Citizens' Action Committee is up for renewal before a public meeting to be held on Tuesday night in the City Hotel. If we don't get inside the walls of the city today, on Tuesday we will take over the old city and hold a public meeting right in the centre of it.'

Canavan's commitment pleased me, but I remained dissatisfied: 'The route banned by the minister is the route the people will want to march. If they are frustrated, they may decide to go it alone.'

'You must hold the line today for as long as you can, but if they want to move against the police and can't be stopped, it's important that you give the order to charge. They have been leaderless for too long. If you give the order, I will go for the nearest policemen.' Canavan replied.

As I left the house, Eileen Canavan took up the hose to wash down the car. Laughter rang out as the water sprayed off the car, scattering the young Canavans.

I checked in with my own family before going to the meeting of the Citizens' Action Committee and tried to persuade one of the older boys to remain at home during the march. John L., Hugh, Declan and Kieran all refused. I then turned to the girls. Roisin and Eileen turned me down flat. The possibility of serious trouble, resulting in injury or even death, was uppermost in my mind and I had great difficulty getting Eileen to promise to remain at home. The youngest child, Nuala, was only three months old, and there were six others under sixteen. Satisfied that there was someone there to deal with an emergency, I headed for the meeting.

The uncertainty and indecision at the Citizens' Action Committee meeting on the previous evening had been caused by the possibility of arrests, as well as a lack of precise knowledge of how many people would be prepared to answer the committee's call to march, ban or no ban. When the action committee assembled in the first-floor office of Brendan Duddy's restaurant on the morning of the sixteenth, our numbers increased by new deputies, no one had any clear proposals to make. The leadership was wrestling with a classic dilemma: how to reconcile peaceful protest with breaking the law by violating Craig's ban – something which could, in turn, provoke a police reaction. The two previous protests – the sit-down in the Guildhall Square and the march by the committee members – had built up support for us. We had also provided time and space for the government to move in the direction of our demands. It hadn't. Its first written response was couched in archaic language and typified its obduracy: 'Thou shall not hold a march or meeting within the hallowed Walls of the Ancient City of Londonderry.'

The length of the ban – it was to extend until four days before the loyalist marching season was due to begin – indicated the contempt in which Craig held the citizens of Derry. The possibility of a head-on collision between the police and the marchers was becoming a certainty. I sensed a disaster in the making as the uninspired rhetoric swirled around me in the upper room. I had asked the marshals to meet me for a final briefing at the back of the Guildhall an hour and a half before the start of the march. The meeting dragged on until I was already late. After having received messages that the marshals were becoming impatient, I prepared to leave. I asked Ivan Cooper to relay, as quickly as possible, any decisions which the Committee might make. I then left the building, thinking that

Canavan's definition of my role – to keep the peace at all costs – appeared to bear no relation whatsoever to the reality of the situation.

An anxious crowd of marshals greeted me on my arrival. Right away they began demanding instructions and explanations. Playing for time, I outlined what I believed was the strategy of the Minister of Home Affairs and pointed out that, if the marchers were seen to be the aggressors, the government would use the full weight of its forces against them. The authorities would then proclaim to the world that the demand for civil rights was only a cover for a conspiracy of Republicans, communists and anarchists. Briefly I sketched my own spontaneous and tentative strategy for keeping the peace. I recommended that we keep about a hundred yards between the vanguard of the march and the police barricades. After organising the marchers and policing the route, all marshals were to make their way to the head of the parade as it approached Craigavon Bridge. It would require a determined effort by the marshals to hold the line of the march because it was certain that those bearing grudges against the police would also have made their way to the front of the parade, determined to repay in full the brutality shown them by the police on 5 October. I then appointed a dozen of my toughest marshals to patrol the no man's land, to deal with anyone who managed to break the ranks of the main body of marshals. Twice during the course of the briefing, I sent a messenger back to the committee meeting asking for further instructions. None came. As I parried questions from the marshals, Seán Keenan, who had spent many years in prison for alleged membership of the IRA, got to the core of the problem which was uppermost in the minds of those present. 'Will the route set by the Citizens' Action Committee and banned by the Minister of Home Affairs be the route which the march will take today?'

My uncompromising answer appeared to satisfy Keenan. 'As your chief marshal, I will walk the banned route this day. Whoever wishes can follow.'

The public-address system was the key to crowd control, and I gave instructions that no one was to have access to it unless I specifically agreed. The argument was put that some of the visiting civil-rights people might want to address the crowd. 'No one uses the mike without my permission,' I shouted.

'What if Gerry Fitt wants to speak?' someone objected in pursuit of the argument.

'Gerry Fitt is only one of thousands in Derry today; he has no more authority or rights than any other visitor.'

Another objection followed. 'What if he insists?'

Remembering Fitt's speech on a previous occasion, I was not prepared to risk worsening the situation. Not even his status as an MP should give him access to the most powerful weapon in the hands of organisers of this march. 'If he attempts to take the mike, break his arm,' I said. So much for my espousal of non-violent protest.

I had information about the police movements reported to me at regular intervals and quickly grasped Craig's strategy: entrapment. The attack on the civil-rights marchers by the police on 5 October had been seen by television viewers all around the world. The government and police had tried to brazen it out, blaming the disturbance on the IRA and subversives. But there was no way they could refute the charges of brutality, or wish away the images of uniformed thugs batoning defenceless people. Craig had to demonstrate to the world that the actions of the RUC that day had been justified, and he didn't mind sacrificing a couple of hundred men in order to do so. Behind light, movable steel crush barriers about one metre high stood the bait. The police orders were to stop the march from entering the city. The thin cordon, no more than four men deep, stretched across the openings of three streets, and behind them, stacked in armoured vehicles, were their long wooden batons and small steel shields. Man for man they were a match for anyone in Ireland. Upon reflection, however, I realised that today they would be outnumbered, 300 to 1.

People were streaming into the city centre from Creggan and the village of Rosemount, from the low-lying Bogside and comfortable Culmore. Never before in its turbulent history had the city of Derry seen such a concourse of people, rich and poor, the radical and middle-of-the-road, young and old. Doctors with soft, immaculate hands, and dockers, their arms thick from labour, filled the ranks. Priests streamed along with their people. Some were wearing their stiff, white Roman collars; others were not, perhaps for fear of bringing disgrace upon the Church. The women in well-tailored garments were outnumbered 100 to 1 by the mothers of large families in their practical best. Workers – and many who had never seen their fathers work and were doomed to the same soul-destroying inactivity – were in the throng. I counted farm labourers, lean and tough, with leathery skins tanned on the mountain homesteads of counties Derry and Donegal. Students, fired with zeal for change, and more dignified-looking postgraduates were also on the march. The unassuming Neil Gillespie, the unsuccessful Republican candidate in many an election, with board and chessmen in hand, was also there, searching for Eugene O'Hare, the Nationalist Party councillor and chess virtuoso. They must have expected lulls during the afternoon when they would have time for a gentle confrontation. They were political antagonists of many years' standing, but shared a mutual love of intellectual combat in a black-and-white-squared battlefield.

Wealth, poverty, class, political affiliations and social aspirations – none of these were important now. Pure anger was driving the people of the north-west of Ireland. Grimly determined, they had picked up Craig's gauntlet. Like Japanese soldiers preparing for hara-kiri, they had washed and put on fresh underwear. They were anticipating violence and wanted their bodies to be clean, should they be the subjects of medical attention – or autopsy. Later I watched the marching crowd making their way in thousands to the setting-off point at the Waterside railway station, where fewer than 500 protesters had gathered on 5 October. Craig's political future hung in the balance as the world's reporters focused their attention on Derry. They were there with their notebooks. They came from every English-speaking country and from every European nation. The hotels were filled to capacity; bed-and-breakfast houses couldn't cope with the overflow and the taxi drivers were stretched to the limit. Most had come to witness the triumph of justice over injustice, and the spectacle of ordinary people challenging the might of the state. The only way Craig could save his skin now was to manipulate the circumstances and tarnish the good name of the civil-rights movement, which had been carefully built up over the previous six weeks. Only the eruption of a fire-belching head on the righteous, indignant and non-violent body of people could turn it into the dragon he so desperately wanted to slay. The few hundred policemen shuffling their feet in the wan November sunshine were the sacrifice he was prepared to make.

By the time I reached it, the square in front of the Waterside station was packed with people. The crowd stretched northwards along the river and was growing by the minute. Thousands were arriving from the city. As they joined the march, there was a bit of pushing and shoving as those who had arrived early to secure a place at the front tried to hold their ground. The new arrivals were slowly forced to the back. Canavan's newly washed Mini became the focus of our attention. Pat Clarke had installed the public-address system, and it was now parked on the exact spot from which the march on 5 October had departed. The marchers were in a vibrant, determined mood. They didn't impede the marshals, as they struggled to place some semblance of order on what appeared to be absolute chaos. Even the appearance of two senior police officers didn't upset the quiet determination of the crowd. The officers' demeanour seemed to indicate that they too realised that the people assembled before them were the authority now: we were many in number and represented majority opinion in the city. Constitutional government had failed and the people had filled the vacuum left behind. Such was our sense of our own power that, had all the policemen in Northern Ireland been ordered to disperse our march, many of us would have died rather than submit to them. I sensed that the officers had also realised that, if it came to a confrontation, their men would be overrun. Politely, they asked me for leave to read out a formal declaration banning the march. A section of the crowd responded with shouts of derision, but the officer's solemn words had about as much effect on the rest as King Canute's orders had had on the advancing tide. The members of the Derry Citizens' Action Committee lined up in front of the Mini, accompanied by a host of newsmen. In its wake, the largest gathering in Derry in living memory symbolically shook the dust off its feet. I had too much on my mind this time to pay any attention to the buildings in Duke Street.

As the head of the march swung into Craigavon Bridge, I could see black-uniformed policemen in the distance; the wide expanse of the bridge was deserted except for a few courageous photographers working feverishly to record every move in the confrontation between people and state. Craigavon Bridge had replaced the old Carlisle Bridge, and had been renamed to commemorate one of the founders of the statelet, Lord Craigavon. The noble lord would have turned in his grave had he been aware of the purposes of those marching along the bridge which bore his name. Watching from my vantage point on the roof of the

Mini, I waited until the main body of marchers had filled the bridge before slowing and stopping the march in its tracks so as to allow the stragglers to catch up. Ordered to halt the march, the marshals, now three deep at the front, braced themselves, and despite the pressure from behind, they brought the crowd to a halt. No one had briefed me about the strategy to follow in confronting the police; as I watched the members of the DCAC move towards the barricades, I wondered what the hell was going to happen. One thing I was sure of: as I watched the huge crowd now packing the bridge from one cast-iron balustrade to the other, I knew that Northern Ireland would never be the same again. Previous demonstrations had given the marshals valuable experience, and the demonstrators themselves knew the value of discipline when it came to putting maximum pressure on the police. The singing of the American civil-rights anthem 'We Shall Overcome' reminded me of the closing hymn of the men's annual religious retreat. Our commitment to our cause here also bordered on the religious. Other marchers sang the slightly more martial 'We Shall Not Be Moved'. This carried a different message, with a promise of action. The voices of some twenty thousand people rent the air and the marshals relaxed as the police grew tenser.

The civil-rights leaders had already begun negotiations with the police at the barricades. I waited anxiously, still without any inkling of what strategy I should pursue. The marchers were becoming impatient as they pushed forward. 'Ah, sit down, sit down,' someone shouted, and the pressure eased. Neil Gillespie and Eugene O'Hare flattened their chessboard on the pavement and took out their pieces. Now and then, a solitary figure would slip beneath the outstretched arms of the marshals and head for the police, only to end up in the hands of the stewards patrolling the no man's land between the head of the march and the police barricades. No progress was being made at the long metal negotiating table, and the tension was rising again. There were shouts from the marshals as they leaned backwards against the surge of the crowd. They staggered forward a couple of yards, then regained their balance. Patience was wearing thin and time was running out. Each new surge tested the marshals to breaking point. I felt panic rise in my throat as I looked beyond my first and only line of defence and saw the angry faces and heard the demands to let the march proceed. Abuse was being hurled at the leadership for its lack of courage. People were shouting at us, demanding that we stand aside and allow the confrontation between police and people to begin. I remembered Canavan's advice from earlier that day: 'Don't let them go it alone.' The marshals were weakening. It was time to give the order. From where I stood on the top of the Mini, I looked down to the bonnet and then to the surface of the bridge, hoping for a head start when the charge began. Turning to the marchers, I appealed for silence. The shouting continued for some time but gradually faded to a murmur. A man who hadn't gambled since he lost his wedding money on two greyhounds, I was about to play the only card I had left in the interest of peace.

'We can take the police,' I boomed out over the PA. With a gigantic sigh, the murmuring ceased.

I paused for effect before continuing.

'We can take the police,' I repeated, 'in two minutes or in ten minutes or in two hours. The choice is ours.'

There was a tremendous roar from the marchers and an immediate release of tension. The pressure on the stewards eased and they straightened up, relieved.

Having captured the attention of the crowd, I spelt out our options. 'Only 200 policemen stand between us and the route we have mapped out. They can be swept aside, when we like, how we like. The choice is ours. But the future of William Craig hangs by a single thread. If we take the police, his prediction that this march would lead to violence will have been vindicated. If we don't, he is finished as a politician.' Craig was the politician most hated by Catholics in Northern Ireland. The mood of the marchers changed and I breathed a sigh of relief. I hadn't resolved anything, merely bought some time. But it was enough. Up in front the civil-rights leaders decided on a token breach of the police barricades. The policemen moved aside to allow the symbolic act to take place and moved forward again to help those who, because of age or physical inability, were unable to scale the barricade unaided. Neither I nor the marchers could see the symbolic act, but the feeling that something important was happening pervaded the crowd and their mood changed to one of expectancy.

I felt a tug at my trouser leg and looked down with shock and amazement at Eileen, standing right in the path of impending disaster. I had left her minding the family. 'What in God's name are you doing here?' I hissed.

'Shut up and listen,' she said. 'None of the gates of the old city are manned by police – the city is there for the taking.' Ivan Cooper, returning from the barricades, addressed the crowd and asked them to proceed to the Guildhall along the footpaths. I ordered the marshals to the barricade to form a buffer between the police and the marchers. Leaving the centre of the bridge free, the front of the crowd diverted to the footpaths and moved forward. Without knowing exactly what was happening, the main body surged forward, ignoring Cooper's request and, like an incoming wave, they flooded the bridge. I had reached the police barricade and was standing on top of a green electric power box, shouting instructions, when the wave hit the marshals and was diverted in the direction of John Street, clear of the police lines. The momentum remained unchecked until the crowd filled the centre of the city, entering it by every gate and opening in the walls. I jumped over the barricade manned by the policemen, who made no effort to intercept me, and headed into the city along the route I had promised Keenan I would take, regardless of the consequences. No one followed, and I felt a bit let down.

A loyalist crowd in Carlisle Road had failed to stop the marchers. In the Diamond, the son of Eamonn Melaugh read out the Declaration of Human Rights, and the crowd cheered the members of the DCAC. The ancient citadel, seat of British power for over 300 years, had fallen to the besiegers without a shot being fired. A newspaper reporter phoned Craig in Stormont from a telephone box in the Diamond. 'An illegal meeting is being held inside the city of Derry.'

'Impossible,' was his reply. Old King Canute had had enough sense to remove himself from the path of the incoming tide, but Craig was swept aside in the most magnificent display of non-violent protest in the history of Northern Ireland.

CHAPTER 7

The City Hotel, unofficial headquarters of the civil-rights movement, throbbed with excitement. Against impossible odds the peace had been maintained. Betty Sinclair thanked me for 'saving a city' and I wondered what would have happened had I pressed the panic button, as I almost did. The real heroes, however, were the stewards, of whom there were about 150: Leo 'Red' Deehan, Paddy 'Barman' Duffy, Joe Coyle, Dr Raymond McClean, John Doran, Michael McGuinness, Pat Johnston and scores of others. Their job wasn't finished either, as Monday saw Craig's ban broken numerous times. All kinds of people waltzed through the gates, jeering and shouting 'SS RUC' at dumbfounded policemen. The protesters demanded a leader for every march, but Ivan Cooper, John Hume and I, and the others, were exhausted. Cooper appealed for a respite. Tuesday was quiet as we looked forward to the meeting in the Guildhall at which we would receive the report from the Citizens' Action Committee.

After the successes of the weekend, the Citizens' Action Committee enjoyed a popularity unmatched by any other group or political party in Derry in living memory. Its members had become household names. Although the liberal Protestant element had been frightened off by the scale of the Catholic antipathy to the government, only the Guildhall had the capacity to contain all those who wanted to identify with and support the people who had taken on the state and the RUC. The government had no idea what to do; the policemen were stunned at the anger and level of organisation achieved by people they had traditionally hated, despised and spied upon. In the end, even the Guildhall could not hold everyone. People spilled out onto Guildhall

Square, where only a few weeks earlier others had sat on wet newspapers.

The civil-rights leaders spelt out the mandate given them at the meeting on 9 October. Michael Canavan opened proceedings. In his analysis of events to date, he wasted no words, added no frills and paused only to allow the audience to applaud our successful moves in the grim game of political chess. Ivan Cooper's address was only a little less warmly received. The crowd applauded him wildly, thunderously stamping their feet. He said, 'We will need this building when we take over control of the city.' Canavan, Cooper, Hume and many others were revelling in their success. Secure in its leadership, the committee could afford to be generous. It did not proscribe any points of view. Seán Keenan, the veteran Republican, had been invited to speak and, towards the end of the meeting, he addressed the crowd. He turned from the civil-rights slogans – 'one man, one vote; one man, one house' – to what he considered the core of the Irish problem. He quoted from a poem by Patrick Pearse, finishing with the words: 'Beware of the risen people who shall take what you would not give, or did you think that life was stronger than man's desire to be free?' It was hard to know if those listening understood the significance of his words, but they cheered, clapped their hands and stamped their feet all the same. The stained-glass windows dedicated to British regiments vibrated in response to the victorious cheers.

I looked down from the platform at the exultant faces, suddenly feeling apprehensive. Keenan had pointed towards the final goal. In the exuberance of the moment, we were like the mice who had 'belled' the cat. The question Keenan seemed to be posing was, 'Who would eventually pull its claws?' In our elation, we abandoned all rational thought; as the evening wore on it seemed as if victory was there for the taking. Emotion enveloped the audience. In their euphoria, people forgot old enmities and made new friends.

I was summoned from the platform and told that a younger section of the crowd had left the Guildhall to go to a factory at Wapping Lane where loyalists had threatened to attack Catholic workers. Hearing that, the crowd – many of them wearing white armbands, the accepted badge of peacekeepers – began marching in formation through the old city. My helpers and I hastened to the factory by a more direct route, arriving just in time to block the narrow street leading into a Protestant area. Some workers leaving the factory appeared to be arguing, but there was no evidence of threatening loyalists. The arriving crowd halted momentarily, then, finding no one to confront, turned immediately to enter the Protestant street. The narrow street, blocked off by civil-rights marshals, became choked with people as the mob rushed to break the cordon. The first charge was rebuffed as the marshals, with arms hooked together, stood their ground. Canavan and I pleaded with the crowd, to no avail. They then regrouped and prepared for a second assault. Realising that they were outnumbered, the marshals unhooked their arms and prepared to defend themselves. Catholics were fighting Catholics in defence of a Protestant area. It was some minutes before the enormity of the situation dawned on the antagonists and a truce was called. This time our pleas for restraint were heeded, and the crowd prepared to leave. The mob scattered in several directions while the marshals shepherded the youngest away from the Protestant area. Relief flooded through me. It was the first time I had seen Catholics display naked sectarianism and I was horrified.

After the crowd had dispersed, grey Land Rovers suddenly poured out of the darkness. They screeched to a halt right inside the square just as the last of the demonstrators were leaving. As the vehicles braked, policemen jumped out and attacked the marshals. I went down on the first rush. As I tried to avoid the flailing batons, I saw Canavan in hand-to-hand combat with two policemen who were bouncing their batons off his arms and shoulders. Michael held his ground. It was all over in minutes: the policemen quickly piled back into their vehicles and disappeared into the night. Canavan helped me to my feet and we went around the square in the darkness, helping the injured. Returning home in the early hours of the morning, I learnt that young Kieran had not returned. The last time I remembered seeing him was when the marshals had hooked arms to brace against the rush of demonstrators in Wapping Lane. We searched frantically for him, finally discovering him in hospital, badly injured. It was no fun being a civil-rights marshal trying to keep the peace in Derry.

Before the end of the month, Prime Minister O'Neill announced his intention of bringing in political reforms. These included the disbandment of Londonderry Corporation and the introduction of the universal franchise. The proposed reforms divided the Unionist Party. Its members argued about things which normal democratic societies took for granted. Ian Paisley wasn't prepared to assist any movement towards enlightenment and organised a counter-demonstration to a civil-rights meeting in Armagh City at the end of November. A busload of civil-rights supporters left Derry early in the morning. Upon our arrival in Armagh, we found that Paisley and his supporters had occupied the city centre during the night. His counter-demonstration constituted an illegal meeting, but the RUC didn't break it up. Instead they ringed the area, keeping civil-rights marchers at bay, while hundreds of Paisley's men paraded with clubs, others singing hymns of praise. I caught a glimpse of the 'Big Man' strutting up and down with his lieutenant, Major Ronald Bunting. Heading for home that night, we shortened the journey by singing the victory anthem 'We Shall Overcome' as we drove through the countryside. Eamonn McCann turned to me and said, 'I hate that song.' I wondered if I would ever understand McCann.

Demonstrations continued in Derry but they would never again match the success of the march on 16 November. Violence broke out, as tail-end marchers began to attack property and the RUC. As the violence escalated, the marshals could no longer function as buffers between the police and those seeking confrontation. The marshals' role as peacekeepers was often ignored by the police and their stock had fallen among a section of the protesters. On one occasion I was caught between two policemen. I struggled to remain on my feet but sank to my knees under their blows as they towered above me, their black uniforms blocking out the sunlight. Driving himself between the two policemen, using his round metal shield to ward off the blows aimed at me, a Sergeant Taylor stepped across my body, which was stretched on the ground, and defiantly faced his own men. Reluctantly, they turned their backs on him as he helped me to my feet.

The civil-rights movement in Derry lost its way, not in one afternoon, but over a number of weeks, as the expectations it had built up were not realised. Initially its leaders tried to pretend that all was well. When they could no longer sustain this pretence, they declared that subversives were infiltrating the movement. This may or may not have been true, but one thing was certain: the pristine non-violent image of the civil-rights movement had suffered. Around this time, the left-wing People's Democracy movement announced that it would march across Northern Ireland from Belfast to Derry. O'Neill had been on television, appealing for all to come together in the interests of Northern Ireland. He formally removed William Craig from power on 11 December. Both the Civil Rights Association and Derry Citizens' Action Committee had suspended all demon-strations. The announcement of the march from Belfast to Derry wrong-footed the DCAC. Its members split on whether to support the march. Most members believed that O'Neill should be given a chance to implement his promised reforms. I was in two minds: I had some sympathy for the Prime Minister but I was not prepared to trust him. In the end, the DCAC refused to support the forthcoming march.

On 1 January 1969, I watched television coverage of the small number of demonstrators starting out on the long march from Belfast. The send-off they received from an angry Union Jack-waving group indicated that they weren't going to have an easy journey. They wound their way slowly across the North, taking long detours to avoid Paisleyites. It was a cold, tortuous walk; news bulletins followed their progress, and showed their latest position on maps.

The tenacity of the young students won them the support of the Catholic population, and forced the DCAC to lend its backing to them. Paisley countered the DCAC's decision by calling a meeting of his supporters for Friday night in the Guildhall. The Council Chamber of the Guildhall was already occupied by Bridget Bond and others, who were protesting about housing. It promised to be one hell of a weekend. My second son, Hugh, dickied up in a white shirt and black bow tie, was preparing with boyish enthusiasm for the annual Thornhill College past pupils' dance in the City Hotel. I left home just before him to join the protest against Paisley outside the Guildhall. Paisley was addressing a large congregation of supporters in the main hall of the Guildhall. Downstairs in the Council Chambers, the homeless Catholic protesters who had occupied the Chamber had barricaded the door and switched off the lights. The Citizens' Action Committee supported Paisley's right to have a meeting in the Guildhall, but tempers were raw in the city and trouble was expected. Marshals were asked to be present. Major Bunting, Paisley's lieutenant, arrived by car and several marshals were detailed to protect the vehicle. During the early part of the evening, the crowd was in good humour and the marshals managed to keep the temperature down. But as the meeting inside the Guildhall dragged on, the mood soured. The crowd began singing a parody of 'The Drunken Sailor':

What shall we do with the Reverend Paisley?
What shall we do with the Reverend Paisley?
What shall we do with the Reverend Paisley
Ear-lie in the morning?
Burn, burn, burn the bastard!
Burn, burn, burn the bastard!
Burn, burn, burn the bastard
Ear-lie in the morning!

Mary Holland, correspondent for the *Observer* turned to me and said, 'There's not much difference in the devils tonight.' The police were out in force but kept a discreet distance.

Suddenly, from inside the hall, we heard the sound of wood being smashed. The gates of the Guildhall were flung open. As the crowd surged forward, they were met by a wave of Paisleyites wielding chair legs and shouting 'No Surrender!' – the war cry of the defenders of Derry in 1689. They cut a wide swathe through the stunned crowd and disappeared into the darkness. Initially, only the people closest to the Guildhall were aware of what had happened. When the confusion had cleared, some began to attend to the wounded, while the rest, angered at what had happened, ran amok, breaking windows. The marshals abandoned Major Bunting's car, which was soon ablaze, the flames lighting up the square. 'Back! Back! It's about to explode,' someone cried.

I retired to the safety of the City Hotel, which by now had become an emergency first-aid centre. People in dinner jackets and evening frocks looked on as bloodstained victims received attention from Dr Donal MacDermott and a host of women.

They used towels and tablecloths to stem the flow of blood; Dr McDermott stitched up wounds with amazing dexterity.

Several sides of Derry had been on display that night. The splendour of the dance, the poverty of the people in the Council Chamber, the bigotry and violence on both sides, the dedication of Dr McDermott and his friends and the courage of Robert Kitson, the Protestant Superintendent of the Guildhall, who – in the face of threats from the Paisleyites – refused to surrender the keys of the Council Chamber, which the homeless had occupied.

I visited the ballroom on the first floor of the City Hotel, and stood for a little while, watching the dancers. The commotion outside grew as the RUC moved armoured vehicles into Guildhall Square. Some dancers went to the window to look. A few of the younger men left their girlfriends to join the confrontation outside, but most of the girls tightened their grip on the Catholic professionals of tomorrow and went on foxtrotting into the early hours of the morning.

It was always difficult to know when Cooper was being serious, but he wasn't fooling this time. I heard him shouting long before he burst into the room. 'The marchers are being murdered,' he screamed.

'What marchers? Where?' someone shouted. Cooper almost fell on the floor, so agitated was he.

'The People's Democracy. Burntollet Bridge.' The room erupted. The marshals who had been planning the afternoon reception went into action. They poured out of the building into any available car and headed off to meet the march. I hit the street ahead of the rest and was across Craigavon Bridge within minutes. As we approached Irish Street, a Protestant area, we ran into a roadblock. 'Put your boot down!' my passengers shouted. As we accelerated, the protesting crowd scattered, bouncing bricks off our cars. It didn't take us long to reach the marchers. I braked hard and ran to help the injured. McCann, who had been travelling in the lead car, ordered me away: 'We don't need your help.' Wounded marchers passed by me, carrying those too badly beaten to walk.

The extremist Protestants had planned the ambush well. Sympathetic builders had left large cones of stones for them on the hillside. Clubs studded with six-inch nails were the weapons they chose for combat at close quarters. The attackers wore armbands for mutual recognition, and handkerchiefs over their faces. Policemen were seen talking to the leaders down in the hollow near the bridge, while other constables guided young students into the gap of danger. The attack was animalistic in its ferocity. The ambushers showered the marchers with huge stones from a distance and, when the students tried to break and run, the attackers moved in for the kill, clubbing the young people, puncturing their flesh. The viciousness would blacken the reputation of Northern Protestants for a long time to come. And for years afterwards, Catholics studied blown-up photographs of the attackers, hoping to identify targets for revenge.

The marchers came under attack again as they passed through the Waterside. Eventually, sore and battered, they arrived at Guildhall Square. Protestant thugs, continuously following the marchers, moved on to the high ground of the old city to hurl stones and abuse over the heads of their police protectors. In Guildhall Square we felt a mixture of horror at the brutal treatment of the marchers and admiration for their courage. Our hearts were filling with hatred of the extremists, and of the police, who had failed to protect the young students. More violence was inevitable and we looked forward to it. Hand-to-hand fighting broke out between the police and Catholic youths and continued for hours. No one gave a damn about peace or marshals now.

There was no holding the young people back. The police station itself came under serious attack. An emergency meeting of the Citizens' Action Committee was called, and it appointed a delegation to seek an immediate conference with the police. At the meeting I insisted on becoming a member of the delegation. John Hume and Ivan Cooper, who normally handled negotiations with the police, were angry at my insistence and suggested that perhaps they were not being trusted. The harness of non-violence was beginning to irk me. I was losing patience with the police, who gave the impression of respecting the DCAC but disregarded them when it suited them. Two senior police officers met the delegation. District Inspector McGimpsey was thickset, with deep black rings around his eyes. I had seen him in action before, on the streets, and he didn't lack courage. In negotiation, his habitual tactic was to stare down the opposition in an attempt to subdue them, before uttering a syllable. His companion was dressed in well-cut civilian clothes, and was much taller, with straight, handsome features and a sallow complexion. I was surprised when he was introduced as County Inspector Kerr. He looked like a man who would have been more at home at a symphony concert. I wondered whether he outranked McGimpsey. I hoped that he would have a civilising influence on the District Inspector.

Relations were very strained during the meeting. The officers made only guarded statements. They contended that the Action Committee had failed to keep the young people in check. We insisted that the police's failure to protect the students had been the cause of the riot. They in turn pointed out that the march couldn't have been protected in the present climate and should not have gone ahead in the first place. They added that the march had proceeded against the expressed wish of the Derry Citizens' Action Committee.

It wasn't an easy meeting, but both sides agreed that it was time for cool heads to prevail. Kerr and McGimpsey promised to keep the police out of the Bogside. The Action Committee agreed to exercise whatever influence it wielded to confine the rioters to the Bogside. I was uneasy as I left the meeting. The policemen had spoken coldly and their promises lacked conviction. I felt that the civil rights movement was like a nut in a nutcracker.

At midnight, I armed myself with a hurling stick and went to St Columb's Wells. After a couple of hours, as I stood there stamping my feet in the cold night air, I began to feel extremely stupid. The rioting had ended. There was no one around save a handful of young men standing about warming themselves at a bonfire on the waste ground. Here I was, alone with my own obsessions, the snow falling lightly around me. It was time to go home.

I heard a noise like thunder. I ran to the door of my house. It was the sound of tramping feet and the tom-tom of batons on steel shields. A mass of black-uniformed figures was moving along the street. 'Fenian bastards, Fenian bastards,' they shouted in unison. My elder brother, Hugh, had to be restrained, otherwise the police might have capped their insults with physical brutality. Every available policeman must have been sent in to assert the force's authority over the Bogside. As they disappeared into the blackness of the night, I remembered my feelings of apprehension after the meeting with the police officers. I couldn't believe they would have ordered their men into an area where the violence had ended.

CHAPTER 8

I slept late on Sunday 6 January. Eleven o'clock Mass at St Eugene's Cathedral was packed as usual. It was difficult to concentrate on prayer. The priest's face kept giving way to that of Terence O'Neill. The carefully modulated tones of the ex-Irish Guard, from a televised speech six weeks earlier, came back to me, drowning out the sermon: 'What kind of Ulster do you want? Do you want a happy and respected province in good standing with the rest of the United Kingdom, or a place torn apart by riots and demonstrations?'

I was caught between respect for the Prime Minister, who despite his background was battling to drag Northern Ireland out of the seventeenth century, and hatred for all he represented. O'Neill's class was, I believed, at the root of Northern Ireland's problems. Yet his courage was undeniable. He had invited Seán Lemass, the Taoiseach, to make an official visit to the North, to the consternation of his less enlightened colleagues. He had sacked the hardline Minister of Agriculture, Harry West, for taking advantage of his ministerial position to purchase land in County Fermanagh. He had sacked William Craig for his mishandling of the civil-rights march on 5 October and subsequent demonstrations in Derry. He had done away with the bigoted and corrupt Londonderry Corporation and had installed an independent commission. He still bore the bruises from a confrontation with the Reverend Ian Paisley. O'Neill had made a point of visiting Catholic schools, and pictures of him shaking hands with nuns had stoked the sullen anger building up against him in the Unionist Party and among grass-roots unionists throughout Northern Ireland. I wondered why thoughts of

O'Neill were interrupting my meditation. The words I remembered from his speech expressed a different and more desperate message than any O'Neill had given unionists in the past. He had told them that if they treated Catholics more fairly, they might learn to live like decent Protestants. I despised him for his aristocratic condescension. His ancestor, Lord Chichester, had seized the O'Doherty lands in Inishowen in 1608. The Chichesters had added insult to injury by adopting the proud name of O'Neill when one of them married a daughter of the clan. O'Neill was reaping what had been sown 360 years earlier. O'Neill's ignoble ancestor had added a wife to his stolen chattels. He now hoped that a new marriage – between the native Irish and their conquerors – would secure the continuation of the conquest of 1608. The noise of the congregation rising to its feet for the last gospel interrupted my historical reverie. I began analysing the conflict in Northern Ireland. Underlying the struggle by Catholics for civil rights, and the Protestant denial that discrimination and oppression had ever existed, lay the ancient and primitive contest between the right of inheritance and the right of conquest. Until that dispute could be settled – or until a greater cause united both communities – no marriage between them was possible. England had occupied Ireland for the purely selfish reason of needing to defend her western seaboard. She was like a third party in the bridal chamber. The marriage could never be consummated while England remained there.

I had been thinking and praying, unaware that another sordid chapter in the conquest of Ireland had just opened. At the cathedral door, I received an unmerciful tongue-lashing from two women from St Columb's Wells who were going into twelve o'clock Mass. 'Where were you last night when we were attacked by the police?' they asked, going on to tell an amazing tale of drunken policemen smashing windows, threatening and terrifying people in St Columb's Wells. I was shocked. I hadn't left the Wells until the early hours of the morning. Except for the boys at the bonfire, there had been no other people around. I immediately headed for the home of James Doherty, a fellow member of the Citizens' Action Committee, to tell him what had happened. The chairman of the Nationalist Party listened to my recital of police misdeeds, and snapped back at me: 'I refuse to believe that the police acted in such a manner. It is an attempt to escalate the tension by irresponsible people.' I looked straight into the eyes of the man I had respected for years on account of his struggle on behalf of the Catholic people. Although we had often differed, my respect for him had never diminished. As I watched the indignation contort his face, I wondered whether his association with the unionist political establishment in various committees and activities had blinded him to the realities of life.

I left James's beautiful Georgian home, which had originally been built as an out-of-town residence for one of the Protestant merchant princes of the City of Londonderry, and headed across the street to a similar building now occupied by a Catholic dentist. I met him at the top of the steps. The dentist had done sterling work as a civil-rights marshal and I felt sure I would receive a better hearing. As I related the details of the police attack on St Columb's Wells, my obvious anger seemed to displease him. I bluntly told him that force would now have to be met with force. I realised for the second time that morning that I was dealing with a materially successful Irish Catholic middle-class leader who would turn his back on me. I slowly turned and retraced my path down the gracious steps.

I was bitterly disappointed, but my spirit was revived by the anger and determination of the ordinary people. They gathered around the Lecky Road, many with iron bars and clubs, thirsting for revenge on the police. Gerry Fitt made one of his powerful speeches. The police had not shown themselves since their drunken sortie into the area in the early hours of the morning. After a heated debate, we agreed to let the women march to the police station and protest, while the men set about building barricades to prevent the police from coming back in. It was left to Eamonn McCann and me to accompany the marchers and to persuade the younger element, anxious now to draw police blood, to remain behind. Peaceful protest and non-violent action continued to be our tactics. As the barricades went up, someone scrawled 'YOU ARE NOW ENTERING FREE DERRY' on the gable wall of a small attic-bedroomed house. The politician's ploy of keeping the people within their own area helped to draw the anger from a very dangerous situation. The erection of barricades to prevent the police from attacking us would have far-reaching consequences. It was certainly not legal. But, as leaders, we gave it our blessing and the people did the rest.

There was no rain, but the January frost was hard. Even in the depths of night, there was light enough from the moon shining in a cloudless sky for the hundreds milling around, waiting for the police to attack. We set up first-aid stations and temporary barracks. Hot soup was available from almost every house, at any time. A pirate radio station played Republican music. Our house was always busy and the family slept very little. Neighbourhood groups set up local defence committees. The Citizens' Action Committee met each night to monitor developments, but its authority was dwindling as new leaders without any qualms about violence began to push forward. James Doherty told me one day that he had seen 'a young person with a pike that could disembowel a man.' The pike was a favourite weapon of the rebels in the 1798 Rebellion, and its reappearance now was powerfully symbolic.

It took five days for the Citizens' Action Committee to restore its full authority, when its plea for a removal of the barricades was finally answered. For five days, Free Derry existed as an autonomous entity. Its existence was at once a major affront to the government, a breakthrough in the political awareness of the people and a dress rehearsal for the future. Paisley stalked the land, condemning the Prime Minister for his inability to defeat the rebels. Firmly in the saddle once again, the Citizens' Action Committee organised a protest visit to London. Washed, brushed and dressed in our Sunday best, we travelled to the Mother of Parliaments. Those who had been injured, molested and threatened by the police on the morning of 5 January were like loyal citizens appealing under the terms of the Magna Carta to the highest authority in the land for redress: 'No one, not even the king or queen, is above the law.' Time would tell whether the RUC was an exception to the rule.

The members of the delegation were in a holiday mood during the journey in a hired bus to Aldergrove Airport. We sang 'We Shall Overcome' with fervour. Some were looking forward to their first-ever flight. A bomb scare delayed our take-off for twenty minutes. Gerry Fitt MP was our host and, in one of the fine halls of Westminster, he addressed us with fighting words. No one could doubt the sincerity of the Republican Labour MP from Belfast. When the Labourites in Northern Ireland were proclaiming allegiance to Britain down the years, he had stood for a united Ireland. The RUC had split many of his supporters' heads when they tried to carry the tricolour through Unionist-dominated Belfast.

In simple, honest language, those who had been abused by the RUC recounted their experiences to MPs. It was a strange occasion. It was almost as if the delegation had come from Outer Mongolia instead of Belfast. We paraded past thousands of unseeing Londoners on our way to Downing Street. Ivan Cooper, John Hume, Molly O'Hara, William Harkin and Molly Barr formed the small delegation which handed in a letter of protest at Number Ten, Downing Street. Hume thanked the police for their courtesy; afterwards we dined in the Irish Club before departing from London. Tired and weary, we returned to Derry in the early hours of the following morning, our duty done. I turned to Canavan. 'Well, what do you think?' I asked. Without hesitation came back the reply, 'We were only one of hundreds of delegations which visit that place every year. The answer to our problems is never to go there again, but to make the British government come to us.'

The tiny village of Moy in County Armagh was hosting a meeting of the northern chapter of the Irish League of Credit Unions. The meeting was called to nominate delegates for the AGM of the movement, which would take place shortly in Dublin. Since Hume was heavily involved in the civil-rights movement, he was taking criticism from those who believed that the purity and usefulness of the movement would be jeopardised by his involvement in street politics. Many of those present clung to the erroneous notion that a movement dedicated to helping people seize some control over their own financial affairs should be non-political. This was a legacy of the paternalism of religious charitable organisations. It seemed to me that Catholics, and some Protestants who were members of credit unions, craved change, but needed to bring it about in an orderly and respectable manner. Hume had some support, and the debate dragged on until the President, Father Gallagher from Clones, stood up. He was held in high regard. A silence settled upon the meeting. Looking around the hall, slowly sizing up the delegates and allowing time for people to settle, the man of the cloth had the final word: 'Ladies and gentlemen, when I started this movement a few years ago, the burden of it frightened me. I saw the potential in it for the people of Ireland, but I trembled at the enormity of the task. There were a number of dedicated but small-minded people around me, and I didn't believe we would be equal to the demand or possess the idealism or ability needed to succeed.' He paused and, in a voice charged with emotion, wrapped up the debate. 'Suddenly from out of the north there came a star.' So Hume was the anointed saviour. I said to myself, 'My God, if he were to die this minute he would be canonised on the spot.'

O'Neill's prestige had been high in December 1969 but by the end of January 1970 he was under pressure from his own backbenchers to resign. He responded by calling an election for 3 February.

Eddie McAteer, the sitting MP for Derry and the leader of the Nationalist Party was a man of absolute integrity and he had given years of service, but the civil-rights movement had pushed him to the margins. The whole political landscape had changed. There was a new sense of unity among the Catholic people which owed nothing to old-style nationalism. Although McAteer had supported the civil-rights movement, he was not closely identified with its success. While trying to urge restraint, he had made a cardinal error by telling us that 'half a loaf is better than no bread', a remark which would be used against him later to great effect. The Citizens' Action Committee, now spearheading the struggle for civil rights, represented nearly all anti-Unionist groupings in the city and had proved far more effective than any political party. The charismatic leadership of Ivan Cooper, and particularly John Hume, who had recently resigned from the Nationalist Party, had created a new semblance of solidarity.

O'Neill had called the election to strengthen his own position within the Unionist Party, but he was also, I felt, aware of the effect an election might have on the various forces for change opposing his government. I became worried. John Hume was ready to catapult himself into Parliament. If McAteer opposed him, Hume, with the civil-rights movement behind him, would brush him aside. But a Hume–McAteer contest would split the nationalist people. If Hume won, he would be lost to the agitation on the streets at a time when he was needed most, and the subsequent recriminations would weaken the people's will to confront the Unionist Party. There was only one means of maximising the gains we had made to date. The chairman of the Nationalist Party, James Doherty, was active in the DCAC and was held in high regard by the public. If he could be persuaded to run in the election for the Nationalist Party, he might win the support of the civil-rights movement and hold the people together. He had spent a lifetime in politics and no one could accuse him of using the movement for his own political ends. Hume would think twice before challenging another leader of the movement. If a political victory wasn't so easily attainable, he might remain with the agitators on the streets.

I talked to Doherty. He didn't buy my arguments: 'If the policy of our party does not satisfy the people, I would not attempt to win their loyalty with a change of leader.' My vision of a two-pronged attack on the government, in Parliament and on the streets, turned out to be fantasy. The Nationalist Party would be in a very strong position in Parliament to deliver on the civil-rights demands; if they failed, the movement on the streets would remain intact and powerful. But if the Nationalist Party were wiped out, the leaders of the civil-rights movement would find themselves sucked into parliamentary politics. If they in turn failed to deliver, we would have nothing to fall back on, and the people would be left confused and divided. I never thought that I would find myself working to save the Nationalist Party. I didn't particularly care about it; what motivated me was a desire to hold together the most effective grass-roots movement in the history of Northern Ireland. 'McAteer can't win in a confrontation with Hume,' I told Doherty. He, who had represented the nationalist people of Derry for many years, replied: 'I feel like an old warhorse who is excited by the smell

of battle. The Nationalist Party will fight and win this election.'
My parting riposte was, 'We will destroy the Nationalist Party.'
So the game was up: the grand alliance of right and left, middle
and working classes, and young and old, forged after 5 October,
had broken up. The new antagonists sharpened their knives.
Northern Ireland's long-suffering minority was in for more grief.

My knife was sharper than most. Despite my reservations,
I flung myself behind John Hume's campaign. Hume's work for
the credit-union movement had established him as a national
figure. His calls for civil rights had captured the imagination of
the people. The electorate had never before unseated an official
Nationalist Party candidate. The National Party's election machine
was intact, and only needed to be cranked up. Eamonn McCann
was the champion of the left and the most articulate of the
candidates. His oratory was both scathing and brilliant. But –
and here I distort one of his electoral slogans – McCann was
not the man.

Our task was to build an organisation, in a matter of days,
that would challenge the historically secure leadership of the
Nationalist Party. It was the moment Michael Canavan had
planned for. He quickly secured electoral premises in Rossville
Hall, adopted the black and white colours of the civil-rights
movement and peppered Hume's electoral literature with emotive
phrases from the campaign for civil rights. We tapped into the
energy of the movement. Workers flocked to Rossville Hall. 'Big
Vinny' Coyle, a successful chandler, temporarily abandoned his
work to take sole charge of our personation machinery. During
the run-up to the election, acting on his own initiative, he
scoured the area collecting the names of people who were sick,
away, or dead. On election day they would all cast their votes
for Hume. Vinny Coyle improvised as no other ever had in the
role of personation agent. He found disguises and wigs for
people so that they could cast multiple votes for Hume.

With a few exceptions, the credit-union activists worked night and day on Hume's behalf. They included Dr Cosgrove, its former President; Paddy Joe Doherty; Brian Duffy; Seamus Bonner and many others. Philip Doherty, a long-term member of the Nationalist Party and Derry Credit Union's most dedicated worker, didn't join us. A wave of change was drowning the Nationalist Party but Hume was nervous right up to the day before the election and we had to persuade him to hold a pre-election rally. He feared that a poor turnout might endanger his chances. It was a beautiful evening and an electoral cavalcade, led by Big Vinny in his chandler's delivery truck, toured the area. I watched the cheering crowds and felt the excitement in the air. I knew then that John Hume would be the new MP for Derry in the Northern Ireland parliament.

Civil-rights campaigners from all over Northern Ireland swept into Stormont with Hume. The Citizens' Action Committee had suspended all business during the campaign. When it reconvened, its members were embittered and at odds with each other after the antagonism at the hustings. The old unity had disappeared. Hume and Cooper resigned from office, and Claude Wilton was appointed chairman in an effort to overcome the divisions. I became vice-chairman.

The new MPs were not cowed by the pomp and splendour of Stormont. They protested by sitting on the floor, demanding instant action. The police were summoned to remove them. Even in high places, excuses were made for the neophytes' behaviour. 'Give them time', I imagined well-bred voices saying. 'You cannot expect those who learned their politics in street brawls to know the traditional procedures and subtle interactions of politics. Give them time.'

As was widely expected, the election spelt the end for the Nationalist Party. It had settled nothing on the Unionist side. With the counting of the votes it was becoming obvious that the

'I Back O'Neill' campaign had failed. What also became obvious was that there was little middle ground in Northern Irish politics. Ian Paisley, in a late run, almost took O'Neill's parliamentary seat in Ballymoney. A series of bomb explosions carried out by loyalist extremists but blamed on the IRA turned the waverers in his party against O'Neill. He resigned on 28 April. Chichester Clarke, a descendant of the man who stole the O'Doherty lands in the early seventeenth century, became the new Prime Minister. After the election of Hume and Cooper, the Citizen's Action Committee had no difficulty in getting a meeting with the new Prime Minster. The arrangements made, we headed for Belfast.

CHAPTER 9

The only previous visit I had made to Stormont Castle was as a member of the cavalcade led by Commander Anderson, Mayor of Derry, which went to Stormont to demand that the new University of Ulster be sited in Derry. I recalled Anderson standing outside Parliament Buildings addressing his fellow citizens: 'We have taken our case to the very steps of Parliament. We can do no more.'

'How wrong he was,' I thought.

As the Derry Citizens' Action Committee mounted those same steps, I realised how much the game had changed. The former Prime Minister, Terence O'Neill, who had attempted to liberalise Northern Irish politics, had been crushed by the intransigent hardliners in the Unionist Party. His deputy leader, Brian Faulkner – to us the quintessential loyalist bigot – had turned on his leader. Following Faulkner's resignation from the Ministry of Commerce and deputy leadership of the party, the two exchanged acrimonious, denunciatory letters, further widening the split in the ranks. O'Neill wrote one particularly bitter letter which highlighted the differences between the Unionists who were trying to cope with a rapidly changing society and those who believed the Union could be preserved only by the exercise of power. It read:

> at no time, in all the difficult weeks since October 5, had you taken any initiative in recommending any measure to take the heat out of the situation. You never came to me, following our decisions of November 22, to say that in your view the franchise must be changed. I had to wait

until I had myself made a positive proposal to lower the temperature, that is, the Commission; and then you produced the two alternatives of doing nothing or of attempting what you must have known to be politically impossible, and therefore, in practice, doing nothing. Hobson's choice!

You also tell me that you remained through what you term successive crises. I am bound to say that if, instead of passively remaining, you had on occasions given me that loyalty and support which a Prime Minister has the right to expect from his Deputy, some of those so-called crises might never have arisen.

Only one who has sat in my chair could appreciate how greatly one is sustained in a difficult and lonely office by the support of truly loyal colleagues. If on these earlier occasions to which you refer, you took issue with me on some vital point of principle, you should surely have resigned. Alternatively, you should have been to the fore in defending the administration. But you did neither. As you yourself so accurately put it, you remained.

Finally, you speak of the party tearing itself to pieces and the work of your department being imperilled. I ask you to consider this: if you had been willing immediately after 5 October to support me in advocating changes which had to come, instead of talking only in terms of strong government, is it not at least possible that much of this travail could have been prevented?

I was flanked by Nat Minford, the Minister of Education, and Robert Porter, the Minister of Home Affairs. The meeting ran a little behind schedule because the Grand National was being run that day and the Prime Minster was watching the race on TV somewhere in the building. He breezed into the room with his entourage, exclaiming, 'Has anyone backed the winner?' I sat there, amazed. I wondered how he could interest himself in such a banal matter as horse racing when the country was sliding towards civil war. My own life had become joyless since I had immersed myself in the campaign for civil rights. Trips to the seaside with my family were only a memory, and a night out would fill me with guilt. I was applying my obsessive approach to my work as a builder's foreman to the politics of civil rights. I suppose I should have been paying more attention to the important things in life, such as the Grand National.

The ex-major, now the most powerful man in Northern Ireland, flanked by his Minister of Home Affairs and his Minister of Education, took up his position at the head of the table. He had a slight speech impediment, which had earned him uncharitably the nickname 'the Stuttering Major'. Hume and Cooper had joined the deputation, which consisted of Michael Canavan, Willie Breslin, Brendan Hinds, John Patton and myself.

Hume was his usual dignified self, but Ivan Cooper joked and laughed nervously before the serious part of the meeting began. We were anxious to get on with things. Hume, after quickly introducing us to the Prime Minister, outlined a series of complaints. These ranged from the attack on the Bogside by the RUC to the need to provide houses and jobs. Michael Canavan sat silently while his protégé, Hume, set out the framework for debate. I wondered whether this panelled room, in its half-century or so of existence, had ever hosted such a confrontation. Canavan forcefully demanded action against the policemen who had assaulted people in the Bogside. The tension was building in the room. Every time the delegation dug in its heels and demanded action from the Prime Minister, Cooper would try to defuse the tension with some jocular remark. I was getting browned off with Cooper and beginning to see him in a new light. He seemed to me to be siding with the authorities. I suspected that he was beginning to identify with the political institutions of Northern Ireland. Hume was made of sterner stuff.

Robert Porter QC was the Minister for Home Affairs and as such was responsible for the internal security of Northern Ireland. He had reluctantly accepted his appointment to the post by Terence O'Neill. He cut a different figure from his predecessors and was considered a fairer man than them. He broke into our debate about the conduct of the RUC. In a mild-mannered way he explained that it would be wrong for him to institute proceedings against the force until an inquiry into its conduct had concluded. He also pointed out that he would take the final decision on whether or not to prosecute the policemen in question; therefore it would be repugnant to him as a lawyer to become involved at this time. I snapped across the table, 'Is the existence of the Special Powers Act not repugnant to you as a lawyer? Is the imprisonment of men without trial not repugnant to you as a lawyer also?' The tone and content of the questions silenced the meeting. The minister flushed. He possessed more power over the lives of people than any corresponding politician in any other country claiming to be democratic. We all looked at him. The quiet lawyer-politician was obviously stuck for a reply. Eventually he composed himself and said: 'I have no wish to maintain the Special Powers Act on the statute book any longer than is necessary, and I will take steps to remove it as soon as I can.' It was a feeble attempt to defend the indefensible. I felt that I had gone to the very heart of Northern Ireland's problems.

I cursed inwardly as another of Cooper's interjections once again took the heat out of our discussion. The moment of confrontation now past, the left-wingers on our deputation – Breslin and Hinds – pleaded for houses and jobs as a means of preventing trouble on the streets. Wearying of the cringing attitude of the two delegates, I rudely interrupted them and declared to the Prime Minister: 'Unless you acknowledge the right of the nationalist people to seek the unity of this country, all the houses and jobs that could be provided will not solve the difficulties of Northern Ireland.'

'Chi-chi' instantly turned his attention to me. We stared at each other. I continued: 'Unless you learn to rule this country justly, we will not allow you to rule it at all.' True to form, Cooper then intervened once again. At this point I ceased to have any interest in the meeting.

That weekend, frustrated at their politicians' inability to deal with the unrest, loyalists took to the streets to wreck and riot. So fierce was the rioting and so severe the damage caused that Chichester-Clarke made an appeal for calm and restraint on television. I watched his long, strained face as he spelt out the options facing Northern Ireland. By way of a peroration he declared: 'If I am not allowed to rule this country justly, I will not rule it at all.'

The election had solved nothing. Intermittent rioting rocked Northern Ireland. The place was becoming ungovernable and the world was watching.

On 19 April 1969, to everyone's astonishment, the RUC fired live rounds during rioting in Derry for the first time. A crowd of rioters, which had been closing in on half a dozen policemen in a cul de sac off William Street, stopped its advance momentarily. Up to now both sides had followed a code of conduct which did not allow the use of firearms. When the shots suddenly rang out, someone shouted, 'They must be blanks.' Another shower of stones filled the air as the rioters moved forward again. Suddenly the shout went up: 'They're real bullets! Some people have been shot.' Indignation swept through the crowd, as it does through spectators at a football match who have witnessed a particularly bad foul. 'You dirty black bastards!' they yelled. It didn't occur to anyone (except the hard-pressed constables) that a few hundred rioters against six policemen might constitute an unfair fight. One of the wounded men was carried into William Street, blood pumping from his ankle. I stopped a car driven by Dr Jim McCabe, who took the victim to hospital. This sinister turn of events had a sobering effect on the crowd. It started to disperse. The police tried to take control of William Street, but as subsequent events would show, they were not even in control of themselves. The hail of missiles petered out like an April shower as the police chased the rioters past the home of Sammy Devenny. Why they then turned their attention to the Devenny home was hard to understand. They may have been following some of the rioters who had fled into the house and over the backyard wall. If so, they didn't catch them.

The policemen turned on the defenceless Devenny family, lashing out right and left with their batons. Sammy Devenny, a big block of a man, took a blow to the head that sent him crashing to the ground. The policemen continued to beat him as he lay there in a pool of his own blood, then turned on his daughter, who flung herself on top of her father to protect him. A senior policeman, holding his polished blackthorn stick, watched while rank-and-file officers beat Devenny to the point of death. Word spread that Sammy Devenny had been killed by the police, and the rioting worsened.

I glanced at Butcher Gate, which had traditionally been the entrance to the old walled city from the Bogside. There was a time when these gates were closed against our forefathers. But as the colonists became more confident in their own power, the Bogsiders were allowed into the city to perform chores or to bring in meat and vegetables for the colonists. The curfew bell would ring and our ancestors would hurry out back to the tiny cabins built in the bog or on the site of the old Franciscan Abbey to the west of the settlement. I shook my head to dismiss the past.

The gate was blocked by a phalanx of uniformed figures. Their shields were raised against the stones the crowd of youths on the face of the hill was lobbing at them. The policemen were big and tall, many standing over six foot. Their long black greatcoats and helmets gave them an anonymous and frightening appearance. I sensed their mood change as they tightened their ranks and raised their shields chest-high. This tactic was as old as history: closed ranks surrounded by steel, short swords or short truncheons for close combat. It was all the same. The rioting crowd also sensed that the policemen had found new heart, and felt afraid. They stopped advancing. The police started beating their shields in rhythm with the tramp of their heavy boots. The thump of truncheons on steel heralded their advance. Arrogance, born out of years of privilege and recent successes, propelled them over the crest of the hill and down into the Bogside. I had seen this manoeuvre before; its purpose was to drive the Fenians back into the Bogside. No arrests would be made now, but next morning the RUC would raid the labour exchange, where most of the rioters would be signing on for unemployment benefit. Prison sentences would quickly follow.

Before the policemen had advanced even twenty yards, the young men had taken to their heels, leaving the stone-strewn battlefield to the pursuers. Then, suddenly, as if obeying a command, the fleeing figures stopped dead and turned to face the policemen. The latter, now out from under the gate, were vulnerable to the stones flying at them in high arcs, showering their helmets and shoulders. As they raised their shields to protect their heads, a second volley hit them at knee level, and they fell in rows, like wheat before a scythe. Panic seized the RUC men; they retreated, dragging their injured with them into the old city. Our respect for the police was long gone; on this day our fear of them also disappeared.

While surgeons fought to save Sammy Devenny's life, an utterly insensitive RUC occupied the Bogside, in its biggest show of strength since the Troubles began. They stood, black and sullen, at the corners of each street, the butts of their heavy revolvers exposed for a quick draw. It was hard to know what they hoped to achieve. They had lost the battle for our hearts and minds a long time ago; the people were beyond intimidation, and jeered at the armed occupiers. Another public meeting was called. Within hearing distance of the police, we decided to evacuate the area for a few hours. If they didn't leave in the meantime, we would return to drive them out.

Hastily strapping young children into prams, jeering all the while at the police, the women led the evacuation. I was appointed to remain behind to ensure that all the tiny houses were emptied of people. In their hundreds, people headed for the heights of Creggan to hold a meeting and prepare for battle. The police remained silent and waited. I kept watch for the next two hours. Only the policemen, clinging like black beetles to the gables of houses, disturbed the silence. Father Mulvey drew up in his car. Seeing that violence was on the cards, he went off to phone the Minister of Home Affairs. It was a race against time. I didn't know what had been said at the meeting in Creggan but I could guess: in the distance I could see a horde of men marching down the hill. They were armed with cudgels and obviously determined to drive the police out of the Bogside. The policemen adjusted their belts so that their revolvers were to hand. Father Mulvey returned. Yes, he had got through to the Minister. No, he didn't know if his advice to pull the police out of the Bogside had been accepted. I noticed some movement among the policemen. Some appeared to be arguing with their officers. Suddenly, they turned their backs on the oncoming marchers and, with looks of dejection, they headed for the gates of the old walled city. Next day, the press carried photographs of the policemen, their backs turned to the cameras, their shoulders bent, as they made their way to safety. One banner headline summed it up succinctly: DEFEATED.

A priest from St Eugene's Cathedral came to my door. He had never paid me a visit before. The tall cleric lowered his six-foot frame into the armchair. I wondered what he was doing here. 'You people are going to get somebody killed if you are not careful,' he said. 'I watched that rabble of people gathering in Creggan yesterday, waving sticks and threatening to drive the police out of the Bogside. There was neither order nor discipline, and a dozen armed policemen could have routed the lot of them. If you are going to take on the police, there is no point in herding the people like cattle, into confrontation where they will be cut to pieces. Tactics have to be planned and carefully worked out.' I listened in amazement as the priest continued: 'When you have the numbers, a pincer movement is preferable to a frontal attack, and a blow from a stick is not as effective as a sharp thrust to the eyes or the throat.' It was a brief meeting, and when the priest rose to leave he said: 'Keep in touch with me by phone. Just ask for Owen Roe.' Owen Roe O'Neill was the legendary Irish leader who had defeated the English at the Battle of Benburb in 1646.

It was a long, hot summer. The main action alternated between Derry and Belfast. On 12 July, Orangemen paraded throughout Northern Ireland to celebrate the victory won by the forces of William of Orange over the Jacobites and the Irish in 1690. Their triumphal marches raised the political temperature still higher; rioting became widespread and every day Catholic families feared for their lives. Many who for years had lived at peace with their Protestant neighbours packed their belongings and fled. In Derry there was near-panic in the Catholic homes nestling beneath the walls of the old city. Father Mulvey purchased two houses in Clarendon Street with a loan from Derry Credit Union and initiated a crash building programme to convert them into flats to house the families most at risk. The age-old divisions between the Catholic Irish and Protestant British widened. In retaliation for attacks on Catholics by marching Orangemen in Belfast, the young people ran wild in Derry. This time, no civil-rights stewards stood between them and the RUC. There were grim, ugly scenes, and for the very first time Derry witnessed widespread looting. Condemnation of the destruction came from both sides of the sectarian divide and was echoed by the Citizens' Action Committee. Then, on 17 July, Sammy Devenny died.

The house in William Street which had played reluctant host to the marauding policemen during the April riots became the focus of attention. Fifteen thousand people watched as the flower-covered coffin containing his remains was carried into the street. Gently the marshals eased the crowd back to allow Charlie Bradley's black hearse to start the one-mile journey to the city cemetery. On the day before, Phyllis Devenny had pleaded for peace and begged that her husband's death should not become the occasion for violence. The ultimate form of violence had been visited on her and her nine children. Women cried silently while men kept their sorrow and anger hidden as they lined up eight-abreast behind the hearse. The DCAC had told the RUC to keep away from the funeral cortège and even turned down their offer to control the traffic that day. With controlled grief, the Bogside buried Sammy Devenny. The RUC protected his killers. An investigating officer from London met a wall of silence. He discovered that pages had been torn from the headquarters' daybook. The force refused to allow anyone to take part in an identification parade. A doctor wrote 'heart failure' on the death certificate. The officer who had marked time with his blackthorn stick as the blows were showered on Sammy Devenny destroyed the reputation of a police force with his silence.

John Hume and Ivan Cooper, the two most powerful members of the DCAC since their election to Parliament, had begun to distance themselves from the Citizens' Action Committee. The divisions caused by the election weakened the committee still further: it was no longer the force it had been the previous year. Hume was a shrewd judge of human nature and possessed a sense of history. He was learning to fill the role of hero/saint – something which, throughout history, the Irish people had demanded from its leaders. His attitude to the people, especially those still engaged in agitation on the streets, was one of peevish annoyance: 'If only they would cease their activities and have faith, I would solve the problems of this country.' Christianity, he said, had never been tried, and the only thing wrong with democracy was that it was in the hands of the wrong people. He proudly declared that he would ride both these horses to victory. He soon discovered that the chariot of the civil-rights movement was hitched to tigers, instead of horses.

The 'Twelfth' was celebrated throughout Northern Ireland, but the Protestants of Derry had another victory to celebrate. The historian Lord Macauley once described the Siege of Derry as 'the most memorable in the annals of the British Isles'. In normal circumstances, the celebrations created a tense atmosphere in the city, but in the volatile atmosphere now prevailing in Derry, the worst was expected. Catholic Derry rested its hopes in the DCAC. The committee was mainly concerned with the rising tide of violence and the lack of movement on political reform. The crunch came when we tried to have the 12 August celebrations cancelled and Paisley threatened to march through the Bogside. His lieutenant, Major Bunting, even promised to troop his colours in the area. Sophisticated political debate was no good against the blunt weapon of bigoted Orangeism. Seán Keenan saw the need for positive, constructive action. He knew that the almost defunct Republican movement now had a perfect opportunity to re-establish itself. Republican old hands like himself had played a small but important part in the civil-rights movement. Keenan put his cards on the table. He sought a meeting with the Citizens' Action Committee and forcefully told them that we would need to make preparations to defend the area in the event of an attack by extreme loyalists.

The threadbare alliance between pacifists and activists in the DCAC was breaking apart. Some hated Keenan and all he stood for, but he did present them with the opportunity to wash their hands of a problem they no longer had the stomach for. I was suspicious of Keenan's expression of indignation, and doubted his sincerity. I was pretty sure, though, that the DCAC was being undermined. But so what! It had been a long, hard struggle over the past ten months. I knew that the DCAC was finished. It had served its purpose; it had roused the people to un-precedented levels of idealism and sent the government reeling in a series of brilliant political manoeuvres, but it was going to suffer the inevitable fate of such movements. It wasn't thorough-going; it wouldn't go for the jugular vein of the establishment and would end up as yet another buffer between the people and the government unless it was radicalised or destroyed.

Keenan scheduled a meeting of concerned citizens for the weekend. He invited the DCAC to send two representatives. The DCAC agreed to meet the following evening to deal with his request. I knew they would take the bait and decided not to attend the meeting. I needed a rest. I would have a night in at home – the first for many months – and an opportunity for reflection.

The election of a number of civil-rights leaders – including John Hume and Ivan Cooper – to Parliament had been the high-water mark of the civil-rights campaign. The Nationalist Party had been swept aside by the new movement. I struggled to understand why people like Eddie McAteer and James Doherty, who had been so vehement in their condemnation of the Unionist Party, were eventually absorbed into the system. These men were totally dedicated and of the highest integrity, and they had endured a great deal, but we had to push them aside in order to let the people speak. But the people's voice was barely audible. It was almost as if they were trying to make themselves heard through the wrong end of a megaphone.

I had noted Hume's and Cooper's reluctance to get involved in debate within the DCAC. Although they were still members, there was a certain aloofness about their manner. They seemed to want to convince us that they could solve all the problems, if only they had a free hand to do so. 'Well,' I chuckled to myself, 'let them sort out the problems. They fought long and hard to get into the driving seat.' I was washing my hands of the DCAC.

The political process had always fascinated me. When, after an ideological confrontation, one leader replaced another, he always seemed to make the same mistakes as the man he had deposed. The rise and fall of leaders within my own community was also indicative of the unchanging nature of politics. I remembered how J. J. McCarroll gave way to Paddy Maxwell in the 1940s. Then, after a spell of bitter antagonism, our newest hope, Eddie McAteer, ended the political career of Maxwell. I had played a leading part in the displacement of McAteer and had endorsed Hume and his deputy, Cooper. Would the process repeat itself, and if it did, who would be the man to upset Hume? Eamonn McCann had outstanding leadership qualities but he had moved so far ahead of the people that they were afraid of him. He had also challenged their strict Catholic value system. It would be a long time before people fell in behind him.

My reflections were interrupted by the arrival of Dr Donal MacDermott. He said, 'You have been appointed, along with

Dermie McClenaghan, to represent the DCAC on the new Defence Association.' I swore out loud as I realised that my absence from the meeting had brought about the very thing I had tried to avoid. I tried to analyse my feelings while the doctor explained the reason for my appointment. I was in a dilemma: I wanted to bring about change and yet I felt the pull of my conservative background. If I had really wanted to get off the stage I should have gone to the meeting and flatly refused to get involved in what was bound to lead to an escalation of violence. In some strange way, I had let the other members of the DCAC off the hook on which I was now impaled.

Keenan's choice of venue – a small community hall in the Brandywell neighbourhood – was a clever one. He could not muster much support in most areas of the city, but he was popular in the Brandywell, an area he knew intimately. He had suffered internment without trial and had spent many years behind bars. He could have spent those years with his family if he had renounced his political views or promised to behave as the state wished him to behave. The laws under which he had been imprisoned had been introduced with the establishment of the state half a century before and had remained on the statute book ever since. They permitted the authorities to imprison without trial anyone whom a servant of the state believed was even contemplating a crime. Keenan was an old-style Republican and his political philosophy was simple: drive the British out of Ireland and let the Irish settle the outstanding issue by themselves.

When I entered the hall, the platform party was already seated, with Keenan in the centre. Except for him, those on the platform were little-known. I knew they were Republicans of one kind or another but they held no significant stature in the community. The Republican movement had been quiescent after it had abandoned the border campaign in the 1960s because of lack of public support. I interpreted the meeting as an attempt to capitalise on the state of fear and confusion among Nationalists. I understood the intrigue upon which Keenan and his friends had embarked; my devious mind followed it with interest. Despite my tiredness and annoyance at being selected *in absentia* as a DCAC delegate, I started thinking about usurping the usurpers. Keenan had the most power within the group, so I made up my mind to keep close to him.

There were more than a hundred people present when the meeting started. They filled the hard, backless timber forms which were normally used for bingo. The overflow stood at the back. Keenan opened the meeting with a summary of the political events that had led to the present crisis and the need to prepare the defence of the area. Even though Keenan was operating in home territory, many people began to display considerable resentment toward him. The people identified Republicanism with armed force. Keenan might have been known as the 'Gentle Republican' but he was willing to fight and die for a United Ireland. I also appreciated their anxiety, for the language Keenan was using was a long way from the words of 'We Shall Overcome'. Seán deflected the criticism by stating that there was no question of the Republican movement playing a political role. He said he was the only Republican on the platform and was acting in a private capacity. I didn't really believe him and was amused at the injured tone in his voice. This group, continued Keenan, pointing to those around him, had come together motivated only by the impending danger and nothing else. They were an ad hoc committee with no pretensions to any kind of authority. They would willingly resign and allow those present to elect a more representative committee, he announced.

Cries of support for the group on the platform came from the audience, while others demanded that additional members be nominated from the floor. The second motion was carried.

Many of those elected from the floor were people with impeccable records of service to peace and the civil-rights campaign. Their integrity strengthened Keenan's mandate. He and the Defence Association had almost acquired the image Keenan wanted and needed. The Derry Citizens' Action Committee disappeared almost beyond trace that evening. Seán Keenan was appointed chairman of the Bogside Defence Association. He reiterated his desire to maintain peace on 12 August. To this end, the committee agreed that stewards would prevent any attempts by Catholics to attack the Orange parade.

The fact that the Citizens' Action Committee had already commissioned a large body of experienced marshals was ignored and Keenan set about the organisation of a new body under the direct control of the Defence Association. I watched carefully as Keenan manipulated the proceedings. I wasn't surprised that in the middle of nominations for the post of chief marshal, Keenan interrupted the procedure to praise the abilities of Len Green. Len Green was a very kind and affable Englishman who had arrived in Derry in a submarine some years before. He had married a Derry girl and settled in the city, and was raising a family there. He had fully and successfully integrated himself into the community. Keenan's strong efforts to have him appointed chief marshal, I believed, were more an attempt to display his own liberal qualities than an expression of faith in Len Green's organisational abilities. I sighed with relief. As acting chief marshal of the local civil-rights movement, I was the most experienced person present, but I didn't want to be burdened with the task of policing the Orange parade. I was more interested in policing Keenan.

The election of the additional members to the committee seemed to allay the anxiety expressed earlier in the meeting, and the organisation of the defence of the area began. This was the first of many meetings chaired by Keenan. The old warrior had the scent of battle in his nostrils and was in his element. As the date drew nearer, people's anxiety increased. Knowledge that we would not be able to defend ourselves against an armed attack increased our fears. Outside help was required.

I firmly believed that the Irish government had a responsibility to look after its citizens in the North. I proposed that we approach the Irish government for help in the event of an attack on the Bogside. Keenan resented the mere mention of the Irish government. For over fifty years the Republican movement had refused to accept that a body elected by a section of the Irish people was really the legitimate government of Ireland. He dragged his feet but I pressed the point, knowing that he would not want a fruitless debate on the legitimacy or not of the Irish government. It would have exposed him to the charge of putting his own political beliefs before the needs of the people. He cleverly suggested that if the motion were changed to an appeal to the Irish people, so as not to rule out help from any other quarter, he would support it. I agreed. Delegates were appointed to approach Eddie McAteer and John Hume for help in arranging a meeting with Jack Lynch, the Irish Taoiseach. Keenan and I were delegated to go to Dublin. We left the building as other delegates were being appointed to seek help from other towns in Northern Ireland. Keenan and I went to the City Hotel to await instructions. John Hume found us there.

I watched the two men with interest as I sat with them at a table in the lounge of the City Hotel. It was two in the morning and the last of the foreign reporters had gone to bed. Both men were drinking whiskey. A taste for whiskey and knowledge of the Irish language were about the only things they had in common. Hume was 5'10" in height. His dark, tousled hair tumbled in half-formed waves over his ears and forehead. His dimpled chin added interest to his handsome face. He bent towards Keenan to listen to the older man's conversation.

Keenan sat bolt upright in his seat. His steel-grey, crinkled hair added inches to his 5'2" frame. He was over twenty years older than Hume but the deep lines in his face did not reflect his age as much as from the years he had spent in captivity and the long days passed in solitary confinement.

Hume was a believer in constitutional government. He was cast from the same mould as the great Daniel O'Connell, who had brought relief to the Catholics of Ireland by parliamentary activity but had opted out when the opportunity for revolution had presented itself. Given the circumstances of the time, it was only to be expected that the two would discuss their political beliefs. Keenan's explanation of O'Connell's 'failure' was a thinly veiled attack on Hume: 'O'Connell died a wealthy landowner during the famine years of the nineteenth century, when half the population of Ireland either died of hunger or fled the country. The laissez-faire economic policy of England was used as an excuse for genocide. It was a devil-take-the-hindmost policy, which in crude terms meant that if you couldn't buy food, you didn't eat.'

Despite the seriousness of the conversation, Hume managed a smile, and as his heavy lips parted to show white, straight teeth, I thought of the bones of emigrants scattered across the bed of the north Atlantic Ocean, forming a monument to England's treatment of Ireland. Keenan was a believer in Pádraig Pearse's doctrine of blood sacrifice. I switched my attention to the unsmiling Keenan. I sensed that the man would gladly sacrifice his life to realise Pearse's vision. The two men got down to the business of the meeting: how to involve the Irish government in the defence of the people of the Bogside. It was ironic that the MP and the ex-prisoner were laying plans for what a constitutionalist might well have described as treason.

Hume wished us 'bon voyage' when we parted later. I envied him his education, which had added knowledge and polish to his obvious natural ability. I dropped Keenan at his home at 2.30am and promised to collect him again at 5.30am to be in time for the 9.30am meeting at the office of the Taoiseach in Dublin. I believe that the meeting was organised by Eddie McAteer. I arrived home and lay down without undressing. For the next two hours I mulled over the course I was taking.

I was well established in my work as a senior agent for the largest firm of builders in the area. My sons and daughters were availing of the education that had been denied me. My mortgage was almost paid off. I had a company car. I was president of Derry Credit Union, the largest community bank in the world. With many years of involvement in community work behind me, I enjoyed a high standing in the city. My confrontations with the authorities and police during the agitation for civil rights had enhanced my reputation among the people to such a degree that few ranked above me in popular estimation. I had deliberately avoided the DCAC meeting and I hadn't wanted to be a member of the Defence Association because I saw where it was going. Nothing could stop a clash on 12 August unless the government banned the march, which I knew it wouldn't. Another possibility was that the Apprentice Boys would forgo their celebrations in the interests of peace. But how could they, given the pressure from within the loyalist community for the assertion of ancient rights? I wondered if the time would ever come when the religious and political beliefs of one side could be expressed without the other feeling threatened.

I was working on a new building for the Ministry of Finance. It would house most government agencies in the area. Despite my agitation on the streets, I was still holding down my job. Of course, my activities were not going down well with those in power or with the Protestant community. But the cause of civil rights was so clearly a just one, and the reaction of the Neanderthal wing of the Unionist Party so hysterically hostile, that many Protestants felt embarrassed. The DCAC was the epitome of respectability. Perhaps I was now jeopardising my respectability by joining the Defence Association. I carefully examined the pros and cons of my decision. Two hours later I had everything sorted out in my mind. We were living in dangerous times. The Defence Association was not as organised as it should be, and I felt that any role I would play within it would be an extension of my work in the DCAC.

We set off for Dublin in the early hours of the morning. On our way we disturbed flocks of pigeons and crows cleaning up the droppings left by animals the day before, or pecking at the carcasses of rabbits run over by cars. It was amusing to watch the birds. The crows lifted off in plenty of time and returned with a lazy grace to their feeding. The pigeons waited until the last moment, then, with their wings beating wildly, they scattered hither and thither, causing me to ease up on the accelerator to avoid hitting them.

Although our paths had crossed a few times, Seán Keenan and I didn't know each other well. But as the journey wore on, we came to respect each other. Our relationship would be greatly tested in the weeks ahead. We had much in common. Both of us had been born in the shadow of the old walled city. We both believed passionately in a united Ireland and admired Pádraig Pearse. I had made a study of Pearse's writings and recited some of his poems as we went along. Keenan was confident that the IRA could protect the nationalist people of the North and quoted figures to support his arguments. I accused him of fantasising and pointed out that there was no evidence that Republicanism was organised or that it enjoyed much popular support. At about 8am, we pulled into the Nuremore Hotel near Carrickmacross. The dining room was a mess. Uncollected dishes and overflowing ashtrays left over from a party the night before littered the tables. An obliging waitress cleaned a table and set it for breakfast. We relaxed as we waited for our meal. The chef had slept in and had to be summoned from his abode. I wondered if Ireland was the only country where chefs slept in.

Seán proved to be a more reasonable man than I had expected. As chairman of the Defence Association, Keenan would bear the brunt of the pressure, but I realised that the position of the vice-chairman would be the most important. I appointed myself vice-chairman.

Our meeting had been arranged for 9.30am at the office of the Taoiseach. We had only minutes to spare when I, directed by Keenan, parked the car near Dáil Éireann. I felt tired but was satisfied that I had established a good working relationship with the old Republican. 'I need a shave and a haircut,' mused Keenan, rubbing his dark, silver-tipped beard. 'You won't have time,' I replied, but he was walking with purpose towards the open doors of a barber's shop. We walked in and Keenan settled himself on the chair nearest the door. The barber ceremoniously shook a blue-and white-striped cloth and draped it over Keenan, tucking it gently behind the cotton collar of his Derry-made shirt. 'Trim or cut, sir?' asked the barber.

'Short back and sides,' Keenan replied, 'and give me a shave as well.' I was anxious to make the appointment on time; whether we did or not depended on the barber, who was methodically cutting through Keenan's wiry hair. I gazed around the shop. My eyes came to rest on a long steel bar fixed about one foot from the ceiling. The bar had a series of pulley wheels attached and I wondered what such a contraption was doing in a barber's shop. I didn't have to wonder for long. Having finished his cutting, the barber reached for a circular brush attached to one of the pulleys by an endless canvas belt. He pressed an electrical button and, as the brush in his hands gathered speed, he applied the bristles to Keenan's head. I could hardly believe my eyes as the clippings ascended in a cloud towards the ceiling.

While the seat was in the reclining position and Keenan dozed, the barber ran the sharp razor across Keenan's strong jawbones. Soon the performance was over. Keenan examined himself in the mirror, apparently satisfied that he could decently represent the people of Derry.

We walked the short distance to the office of the Taoiseach. We were ushered into the presence of a tall, austere-looking man. After offering us seats, he sat down and explained that the Taoiseach was unavailable, but as Secretary to the Taoiseach, he had been appointed to meet the delegation. Keenan explained the purpose of the visit. As he raised the scenario of violence in Derry, the man's lips became dry and his face paled. He got even more uncomfortable when Keenan pressed for military assistance in case the worst happened. Whatever briefing he had received had not prepared him for this. But, like all civil servants, he had already prepared his escape route. As soon as Keenan had finished, the civil servant got up and announced that two experts on Northern Ireland were waiting to interview us at the Department of Foreign Affairs. We were ushered to the front door of the building and given directions to our next destination.

The experts were in a relaxed mood as they introduced themselves to us. In a congenial atmosphere, Keenan repeated what he had said to the Secretary to the Taoiseach. Over the next two hours we explored the political possibilities and options for Northern Ireland. The civil servants focused on the success of the civil-rights movement. They believed that if they built upon their achievements to date, Northern Catholics might be able to participate more fully in political life in the North and perhaps learn to accept the permanence of partition. As the meeting wore on, I realised that these experts were expressing the government's real position on the North. Official expressions of support for reunification were no more than lip-service to an ideal. We spelt out our concerns about what might happen during and after the forthcoming march by the Orangemen. They, in turn, tried to calm our fears. Finally I asked: 'What will happen if an attack happens and people are killed?'

'We'll not let you down,' was the suave reply.

'What does "We'll not let you down" mean? Will you protect the people of Derry in the circumstances we have outlined?' I had the bit between my teeth and I wanted precise answers.

'Of course the government will act to protect our people in Northern Ireland,' they replied.

I pressed them further. 'The government is not in session. How will it act?'

'There are enough Cabinet members within a two-hour drive of Dublin who can make a decision, and you will not be abandoned.'

'Can we take this message back to the people of Derry?' I asked.

'Yes,' was the response.

This commitment wrung from the civil servants ended the formal part of the meeting. They wished us good luck. I was not feeling happy after this session. All the same, I could go back to Derry and state truthfully to the Defence Association that we had assurances from those acting on behalf of the Irish government that the nationalist people of Derry would not be abandoned and that, in the event of an attack on the Bogside, the Irish government would take steps to protect the people. As we left the building, Keenan – having faithfully discharged what was obviously a distasteful duty – turned to me and said, 'Let's go and see *my* people.'

We drove immediately to Gardiner Street, where I gained an insight into the utter ineptitude of Sinn Féin and the IRA in this Year of Our Lord 1969. A house on Gardiner Street was the headquarters of Sinn Féin. This organisation claimed to hold a mandate from the people of Ireland, as expressed in 1918 in the last general election in which all the people of Ireland had voted. In that election they had voted for Irish independence and sovereignty.

Keenan spoke in Irish to a young man in the front room of the gracious – if unkempt – Georgian house. The young man, who wouldn't have been born when Keenan last saw action, didn't seem to recognise him. He left the room and returned with another man who was about Keenan's age. He and Keenan greeted each other warmly. Talking in Irish, which I did not understand, they appeared to reach some understanding. Keenan turned and left, with me running at his heels. 'We are to return in fifteen minutes,' he said. We walked the short distance to the Belvedere Hotel, where Keenan ordered a beer and I a fruit juice. 'We are going to meet the commander-in-chief,' Keenan said. 'You'll like him. He has a grown-up daughter but he looks so young and fit we gave him the nickname "Peter Pan".' There was simple pride in Keenan's voice.

As we approached the Sinn Féin headquarters, a car drew up at the kerb. We were ordered to get in quickly. The silence in the car reflected the secrecy of the mission. The man in the passenger seat – our guide – kept glancing back through the rear window. I had no idea where we were going. I might as well have been wearing a blindfold. Finally we stopped in front of a pair of closed gates which looked like the entrance to a builder's yard. As the guide opened the small wicket in the centre, my assumptions were confirmed by the neatly stacked scaffolding, ladders and paint drums. There was an air of organisation to the place. As we stepped over the threshold, we were greeted by Peter Pan's daughter. She was small, slender and well-groomed. She said her father would join us shortly. She directed us to a small office on the first floor of a two-storey building. The office had the usual table, chairs and filing cabinet. What struck me about the place were the posters of Marx, Lenin and Mao Tse-tung. They glowered down from the walls. The posters shouted shrill slogans: 'Workers of the World Unite!' and 'Power Comes Out of the Barrel of a Gun!' One face I had never seen before was that of Che Guevara. I was struck by how youthful he looked compared to the tired old men in the other posters. I turned and pointed to the posters. 'What the hell is all this about?' Keenan shrugged his shoulders and said, 'People from all over the world come to visit here; the posters are probably mementoes they left behind.' It began to dawn on me how little Keenan, the man of the 1940s, knew of the IRA of the 1960s.

When Peter Pan entered the room, Keenan immediately rose to greet him, snapping to attention in deference to the chief. I was introduced to him and we exchanged a few pleasantries. Keenan then cleared his throat. Standing upright with his arms by his sides, in a clear voice he repeated the motion passed unanimously the night before by the people gathered together in a small corrugated-iron building in the heart of nationalist Derry: 'The citizens of Derry call upon the people of Ireland to come to their assistance if the Bogside is attacked.'

The Commander-in-Chief of the IRA was sitting on top of the table, one sandalled foot on the floor, the other swinging freely. I could see his bare toes straining against the leather straps of the sandals as if they were trying to break out. What we heard next shattered a myth. The commander replied: 'I couldn't defend the Bogside. I have neither the men nor the guns to do it.'

Keenan stood there, motionless, as if the message hadn't sunk in yet.

'I told you the IRA was only a myth, a fantasy army, with nothing to offer the people of Ireland,' I sneered. I sat down. The toy soldier, the Commander-in-Chief of the phantom army, was shaken by my reaction. In an effort to retrieve the situation he said, 'But I will have the Chief of Police or the Minister for

Home Affairs assassinated.' My imagination transferred him and his worn-out slogan of assassination to the wall to join the other old men.

'My God,' I exploded. 'As if we didn't have enough problems in Northern Ireland.' Turning to Keenan, I said, 'Let's go back to Derry, where there is work to be done.'

We passed a slogan, 'Give Peace a Chance', daubed in large white letters on the tarmac, as we made our way up Fahan Street towards the Apprentice Boys' Hall in the walled city. While we had been away, seeking help in Dublin, attempts had been made to avert trouble on the 'Twelfth'. These included the distribution of flowers. The peacemakers were suspect in many people's eyes. Their efforts only spurred us on in our defensive work. Our purpose was to make the controlling body of the Apprentice Boys aware of the possibility of serious trouble if the parade were allowed to take place. Their granite Scottish baronial building, with its turrets and high, square battlemented tower, dominated its surroundings. It had been constructed on the site of the old monastic settlement which dated from the sixth century and was the world headquarters of the Apprentice Boys of Derry. The meeting was chaired by Doctor Abernathy, who remained silent during the proceedings, leaving the talking to Jim Guy, the secretary, and the Reverend Dickinson, the chaplain. Politely, they explained the precautions they had taken to ensure that the march would pass off peacefully. We Bogsiders insisted that the only way to ensure that there would be peace would be to call off the parade. They flatly refused.

Returning to the Bogside, we saw two boys with pots of black paint busily obliterating the white plea for peace from the tarred roadway. No one slept that night. Residents scoured the area for material for barricades. The Bogside was now on a war footing. The rancour which followed the election of John Hume was temporarily forgotten as we mobilised against an invasion. In the

Brandywell football ground, I heard Eddie McAteer call on the Irish government 'not to stand by in our hour of need'. Seán Keenan told a large gathering in the Stardust Ballroom: 'We have no guns; there will be no guns. We will attempt to keep the peace, but if we fail, we will defend the Bogside with sticks and stones and good old petrol bombs.' Some of the unemployed were learning how to stop police jeeps with sharpened reinforcing rods for puncturing radiators and how to use specially designed artefacts for puncturing tyres. In the event of an attack, I was to supervise the defence of the area to the west of Rossville Street. That meant erecting three barricades. One was to be built at Abbey Street, the former site of an Augustinian Abbey, and another at the entrance to the Little Diamond, where at election time people in their hundreds would rally to clap and cheer their political leaders. The third barricade was to be placed at Marlborough Terrace, to the west.

During the day, Bernadette Devlin appeared in Rossville Street with a camera crew, causing a stir of excitement. I watched the tiny figure striding resolutely towards William Street and wondered if she thought the peace could be preserved. 'Monsie' Morrow, the local bookmaker, was giving odds of ten to one on peace, but there were no takers. The question was no longer if, but when trouble would begin. Anticipating that the Defence Association would place its marshals at strategic points along the route of the parade, I asked my sons to go to Long Tower Street, which was opposite the Protestant Fountain area and was a potential flashpoint. As the time for the parade approached, I decided to check out other possible flashpoints and found, to my dismay, that the Defence Association seemed not to have made preparations for keeping the peace. I collected my sons and took them home. Eileen asked, 'Has it started yet?'

'No,' I replied. 'What's keeping them?' she said, with impatience. Outside the house, people were lifting the paving

Ann Street, where I was born, with Rossville flats towering in the background. My father is standing on the right of the photograph

Bishop Farren, accompanied by the Bishop of Agra in India, visiting my house, the headquarters of Derry Citizens' Defence Association

Davy McLaughlin from Rosemount had the honour of beginning the painting of the white line which marked the boundary of Free Derry. I'm looking on with Billy Nelis and Phil O'Donnell

January 2001: The most famous gable end in Ireland, still bearing our slogan of resistance

Courtesy Pacemaker Press International

Free Derry in 1969. With Jim Callaghan, British Home Secretary, and Vinny Coyle (in hat)

Courtesy *Daily Express*

A Hogg in our Bog. Greeting Quentin Hogg (the future Lord Hailsham) on his visit to the Bogside in 1969

At the final meeting of Derry Citizens' Defence Association

stones to form barricades. The area stank of petrol. From the old city we heard the sound of drums. It was time to face the music.

Waterloo Square throbbed with the sound of Lambeg drums and the skirl of Scottish war pipes. The square was the nearest the Apprentice Boys' Parade would get to the Bogside during their march. If they chose to troop their colours in Catholic territory, they would have to pass along the narrow throat leading from the square to the Bogside. There the attack would come. The police poured into the narrows and erected barricades. The remnants of the Citizens' Action Committee and their marshals took up positions between the police and the steadily swelling Catholic crowd. 'Monsie' increased his odds to twenty to one. There was still no evidence that the Defence Association had made any attempt to keep the peace. The marchers hurled abuse across the barricades at the Bogsiders, who instantly reciprocated. Stones soon replaced insults, and the battle began. The depleted ranks of DCAC stewards tried to calm things down. Eddie McAteer was their anchorman, his huge bulk straining against the weight of the crowd. Cooper was felled by a stone. Several times the line of marshals broke and re-formed. The policemen behind their vehicles and steel shields held their ground for over an hour. Reinforcements arrived and they prepared to charge. As the engines of armoured vehicles revved up, the Bogsiders cheered. All their planning would not be in vain: the RUC was about to take the bait.

Bernadette Devlin asked me for the loud hailer. Atop rapidly rising barricades in Rossville Street, she addressed the Bogsiders. The peace had broken down. I left to take charge of my own area. Before the barricades had been fully secured, the heavy police vehicles smashed their way into the Bogside, leaving gaps which the defenders had trouble closing. I watched the policemen pour through on foot to face petrol bombs. A direct hit set a policeman's uniform on fire. He screamed as his comrades rolled him on the ground to put out the flames. At the request of a priest, I organised a mini truce with the police in order to evacuate old people from their homes as petrol bombs landed on the roofs. The young Bogsiders stood back to allow an older, more docile generation to pass through. Soon the police resumed the battle, during which the tall, dark officer called Campbell who commanded them would earn a medal for leading his men against the enemies of the queen.

The maisonettes which had replaced the hotchpotch of houses in Rossville Street in the 1960s were four storeys high, with horizontal lines as their main architectural feature. The external staircases were clad with white boards, spaced to allow air to circulate. The young men climbed the boards like cat-burglars and occupied the flat roofs. The buildings – at right angles to the main barricade – were a perfect spot from which to launch an attack on the policemen as they stormed through the breaches made by the heavy armoured vehicles. From a height, missiles and petrol bombs could be lobbed a greater distance. The police fought foot by foot to surround the buildings and cut off the supply of petrol bombs to the roof. Isolated and without weapons or access to the houses below, the petrol bombers engaged in hand-to-hand combat with the policemen, who were slowly dislodging them from their position. Seeing the plight of the young men on the roof, people on the ground redoubled their efforts to clear space for their retreat. They lowered themselves down the long boards. The watching crowd roared. Having only enjoyed limited success on the roofs of the maisonettes, the young men made for the roof of the ten-storey block of flats built to keep a swelling population within the Bogside. From the top of this symbol of gerrymandering they stopped the advance of the RUC into the Bogside.

The several hundred occupants provided support for the front-line troops up on the roof, nearly a hundred feet above the ground; they in turn forced the RUC to retreat to a safe distance. Not content with forcing the withdrawal, they improvised a makeshift catapult. It gave their missiles more range and created another stretch of no man's land. People emptied out of the cathedral onto the brick-strewn streets after evening devotions, just in time to witness a joint charge into the Bogside by the police and loyalist civilians. Father Mulvey angrily ordered an officer to get his men out or 'I will lead the people against you.' Sounds of smashing glass rang out as the police and civilian auxiliaries continued their sortie into the Bogside. I addressed the crowd in front of the cathedral gate: 'Will you do nothing to help? Father Mulvey has threatened to lead the people against the police if they don't withdraw.'

'What can we do? We have no weapons,' they objected.

'Break up the footpaths,' I ordered. Showers of broken paving stones forced the armoured policemen to seek cover. Although the number of Protestants involved in the attack on the Bogside was tiny, it was enough to swing the population behind the Defence Association. What had begun as a riot now assumed the complexion of a popular insurrection.

In Number 10, the operational headquarters of the Defence Association, Eileen was in charge of the action. Food was being produced non-stop. All four rings of the gas cooker were burning. Soup boiled and bubbled in huge pots and a mountain of sandwiches grew as the women of the neighbourhood joined the ad hoc catering corps. What was happening in my home was happening in homes all over the area. The women adhered to their traditional role, while Bernadette Devlin expressed their anger for them at the barricades. She smashed paving stones into manageable sizes. Meanwhile, Pat Clarke was operating a walkie-talkie system and monitoring police communications.

Every room in the house was full. In one, Keenan was directing the defence of the area. People flocked to the headquarters carrying messages, seeking instructions or a bowl of soup. There was scarcely room to move. Somebody arranged for our children to stay with friends. All but the very youngest of them resisted; the rest joined in the frenzy of activity. Elsewhere in the Bogside, barricades were being reinforced, petrol bombs manufactured and stones carted to the front line in mechanical dumpers taken from building sites. We were mounting coherent resistance to the state. The fighting grew in intensity. Casualties were mounting. Doctors from outside the area joined Donal MacDermott and Dr Ray McClean in the temporary first-aid post in a sweetshop, the Kandy Korner. The doctors asked no questions and wrote nothing down. People shut up, got stitched up and got back to the barricades.

Robert Porter, who was born and reared not far from my home, ordered the use of CS gas. Jim Callaghan, the British Home Secretary, had sanctioned this extreme measure a week earlier. CS gas had been used against rioters in the colonies but this was the first time it had been used in Great Britain or Northern Ireland. The RUC pumped round after round of gas into the Bogside. Temporarily blinded, choking and coughing, the rioters reeled under the onslaught. With six other women using borrowed sewing machines in the headquarters, Eileen organised the mass production of gas masks. Kathleen MacDermott scoured chemist shops for cotton wool. When it ran out, people ripped open sanitary towels for filling for the improvised masks. Men placed buckets containing a mixture of water, vinegar and lemon juice outside houses. People submerged the newly manufactured masks periodically in the mixture to make them more effective against the gas. It was hard to say whether the masks really worked or whether people just built up a resistance to CS gas, but one thing was for sure: instead of subduing us, it only stoked our anger and stiffened our resolve. The old and people with chest complaints suffered most and had to be evacuated.

Keenan called a meeting of political and community leaders to discuss the situation. The tiny house was scarcely able to hold the number of people who answered his call for support. The two sitting MPs, Hume and Cooper; the former Nationalist MP, Eddie McAteer; James Doherty, Chairman of the Nationalist Party; Claude Wilton, the liberal Protestant solicitor, and many others filled the front room and hallway while the battle raged outside. The atmosphere in the room was highly charged; some of the people present could not contain their emotions. Claude Wilton was almost in tears as he told us that people would be killed if the fighting continued. Eddie McAteer stated his position unequivocally: 'The situation is totally out of control. I have no intention of getting involved in an attempt to intervene on the streets.' He left the room. He would choose another way to employ his talents and experience. Chaos was now threatening the political system Cooper had fought so hard to reform. He left. Then James Doherty and several others went. Hume, elected leader of the nationalist people of Derry, had kept his opinions to himself. He left, saying, 'Excuse me, gentlemen, I have another meeting to attend.'

Only three people remained in the room: Keenan, Leo Casey, secretary to St Columb's College, the Catholic grammar school, and myself. Keenan looked shattered. He sat slumped in a chair; the possibility of leading a united people against the government had slipped from his grasp. My heart went out to the older man who had suffered so much in the past and who was prepared to sacrifice all for an ideal. I was aware of my own precarious position. The withdrawal of the other leaders had isolated the Defence Association. It would shoulder total responsibility for the confrontation with the police. As Keenan's deputy, I would be treated with equal severity before the law. I examined my options. There was no way back now. I interrupted Keenan's contemplations: 'I'm nailing my colours to the mast. We have a job of work to do.'

Leo Casey, who had not been identified with the rebellion in the Bogside and who could easily have slipped out of the meeting at any time, unnoticed, said: 'Count me in. If we go down, we go down together.' My admiration for Casey soared. His family background, his responsible professional position and his work for Catholic charitable organisations had hardly prepared him for revolution. 'How much money do we have in hand?' I asked Keenan.

'About seventy-eight pounds.'

'My God! What a way to start a war,' I responded, as I headed for the door. I called two men in their early twenties into the room and issued instructions. 'There is seventy-eight pounds available for defence. Buy petrol and, when the money runs out, take what you need and issue receipts for unpaid petrol. The Bogside must not be captured by the police.' Much more petrol would be bought or stolen and used over the next few days. But the fact that an officer of the committee had issued this particular order put an imprimatur on the activities of the rioters and stiffened their resistance.

If the policemen were hoping that the rioting would peter out in the early hours of the morning, as it had often done in the past, they were disappointed. Dawn broke to reveal a tricolour flapping in the breeze on the high flats above scenes of devastation. Two square miles of streets were littered with debris of every kind. Young and old filled milk bottles from an apparently inexhaustible supply of petrol. The police, their ranks depleted by injuries, held their ground beyond the range of the petrol bombers and fired their CS-gas guns at everything that moved. With monotonous regularity the guns could be heard firing their nauseating missiles into the Bogside. The numbers suffering from the effects of the gas increased dramatically. People stopped counting as the number of cartridges fired exceeded one thousand. The cloud of gas thickened and slowly crawled up the side of the ten-storey block of flats. It burned the throats and nostrils of the boys on top, increasing their anger and determination. On the ground, necessity produced leaders. When the boys fell during frontal attacks on the police, they were carried away to the first-aid station and quickly replaced. The rioters were raw and disorganised but they were fast and flexible.

That afternoon, Dr Donal MacDermott and I called a press conference in a community hall in the Bogside. We had gone beyond demanding decent housing, jobs and equal opportunities for Catholics. At the meeting we issued a straightforward call to arms. Loyalists responded to the call and joined the police against us on the edge of the Bogside; others milled around the city centre, easily recognisable with their hard hats and cudgels. The RUC barracks in Rosemount, about two miles away from the main confrontation, came under attack. Barricades were built to isolate the buildings; eavesdroppers, monitoring the police messages, registered the rising panic inside the building. Petrol bombs crashing against the main door were answered by CS gas. John Hume arrived to call for restraint. At an impromptu meeting, the people agreed to send a message to the police: 'Stop the CS gas and we'll take down the barricades.' The radio crackled as the trapped RUC men sought instructions from headquarters. Headquarters responded: 'Promise that bastard anything so that we can get in with reinforcements.' They reached some kind of agreement. Just as the besiegers were dispersing, Hume was struck by a gas cartridge and collapsed. Billy Nelis helped him away.

We heard that Jack Lynch, the Taoiseach, was to address the nation that evening. People began to drift away from the barricades. Donal MacDermott went in search of a television while a packed Number 10 listened to the radio. Lynch condemned the Northern Irish government and the RUC and called for intervention by the United Nations. He demanded that Britain enter into negotiations to undo partition, which, he said, was the root cause of the trouble. His words, 'It is clear also that the Irish government can no longer stand by and see innocent people injured and perhaps worse', were to haunt him for years. Lynch announced that army field hospitals would be established close to the border to care for the injured in Derry. People ran from their houses cheering. MacDermott returned elated and my son, Hugh, ran a tricolour up the nearest lamp-post. The Bogsiders, delighted, returned to the barricades by the hundreds. They intensified their attack on the police. The RUC withdrew from William Street and the rioters filled the gap. Brewster's bakery, now on fire, illuminated the gathering darkness. 'Monty' emerged out of the mist of choking gas in army fatigues with his face blackened. I hadn't seen the former activist for years, and readily agreed to his request for a meeting. Because of the pressure for space in the house, we talked in the hallway.

'I'm at a loss what to do. I have an IRA active-service unit but the politics of the situation are beyond me. We intend to burn out a prominent Unionist tonight but I want to know how you feel about it,' Monty explained.

Here was yet another layer of complication. I was looking at a throwback to the IRA of the 1950s. As I thought about Monty's dilemma, I remembered his leader, the toy soldier who had admitted the IRA's inability to protect the Bogside. I realised the strength of our position. There was no one around to challenge our authority. The prominent Unionist in question was probably sunning himself somewhere far away. 'There may be a caretaker or even a family occupying the building,' I said. 'If you burn it you may cause loss of life.' Monty hesitated. I continued: 'I can identify two targets for you behind the police lines deep in Unionist territory. Destroying them will cause confusion and ease the pressure on the Bogside, without killing anyone.' Monty agreed to burn both.

There was fighting at every barricaded entrance to the Bogside to the north and north-west but it was heaviest in

William Street. The petrol bombs were taking a heavy toll on the buildings separating the Bogside from the police station in the Strand Road. Our walkie-talkie network allowed us to monitor the fighting but it had no decisive bearing on the outcome of the battle between the police and the rioters. Near midnight, Eddie McAteer phoned me and asked me to meet an important visitor to the area. McAteer's home was on the side of the hill which rose steeply from the Bogside. As I reached the top of the steps which eased the steep climb, I turned to look back. The flames from the burning buildings in William Street licked the sky, illuminating the city walls. I looked north towards the targets I had singled out for Monty, but no flames disturbed the darkness.

I had never met Neil Blaney, Minister of Agriculture and Fianna Fail TD for North-East Donegal. He was one of the most powerful men in Ireland. He had been born while his father was a prisoner of the British, under sentence of death, during the War of Independence. The Treaty saved him and 'Old Neil', as he was called, eventually became a TD and a government minister. After his death, young Neil inherited his seat and rose rapidly in the Fianna Fáil hierarchy. He was a master orator, a brilliant electioneer and a firm believer in the reunification of Ireland. I believed that the presence of a high-ranking Irish minister behind the barricades reflected of the Irish government's concern for the Bogside. I felt a sense of relief. I was convinced that the Irish government should take steps to protect the nationalist population of Northern Ireland. What I had seen of the IRA further convinced me of the need for direct involvement by the government of the Republic. I was convinced that the Irish government should now address the task of reuniting the country. Its failure to act had created a vacuum which others would fill. McAteer had been a personal friend of Blaney for years. He introduced the minister, a man with strong, earthy features and quick, intelligent eyes. The meeting lasted an hour. Having fully briefed the minister, I left McAteer's home and made my way back to the steps leading down to the Bogside. I paused once again at the top and looked north. Still no signs of fire. Meanwhile, buildings on the edge of the Bogside were blazing. The sorting office within the Bogside was now in flames. 'Damn you, Monty, you incompetent bastard,' I muttered to myself. Despite my disappointment at Monty's failure to burn the appointed targets and draw state forces away from the Bogside, I felt reasonably sure that we would receive help from the South. Soon I wouldn't need to bother with the IRA. It had been foolish to expect anything from them in the light of what Peter Pan had told me in Dublin.

The Irish army was a different proposition. Although small in numbers, it had made a considerable contribution to UN peacekeeping efforts and several hundred Irish soldiers were on duty in the Middle East. Now was the time for them to make their presence felt in their own country. Blaney shared my belief that the Irish government should become involved and was on his way to Dublin to persuade his colleagues that now was the time. Moreover, the reports we were getting from Belfast, where nationalists were outnumbered, worried us terribly. Over the years Jack Lynch had built up a good relationship with Harold Wilson, the British Prime Minister. Wilson, it was said, believed in the inevitable unification of Ireland and was not trusted by the loyalists. If he could be persuaded to seize the initiative in the Belfast area, the Irish army could handle the west, where nationalists were in a majority and would have welcomed them. A joint occupation would have spelt the end of the northern statelet and perhaps would have led to a resumption of the British-Irish negotiations of fifty years earlier.

Blaney was not the only Donegal man to visit the Bogside during the fighting. Several entered my house, led by a short man who walked with a limp. His chubby, florid face sweated profusely as he made his offer to me: 'Two hundred rifles and a quarter of a million rounds of ammunition are in the magazine at Carndonagh. We have the keys, and the armaments can be delivered to Derry in a matter of hours.' The other members of the deputation nodded in agreement. The arsenal in Carndonagh was for the use of Irish army auxiliaries. I was surprised: during my visits to Inishowen in the previous two weeks seeking help in the event of an armed attack on the Bogside, I had received only one positive response. A contact in Moville had promised a unit of about twelve men, trained and armed with weapons. It would provide token resistance while the Irish government made up its mind. I believed that the Irish people would force their government to intervene in the event of an armed attack on us by the B-Specials. The tactic of allowing the loyalist forces – and I included the RUC among them – to appear as the aggressors had swung world opinion behind the nationalist people. The men from Moville were only to act in the event of an armed attack. This new deputation – tough countrymen with musical accents, so different from the flat tones of Derry – waited patiently as I weighed up my options. It was one thing to resort to armed resistance to defend the people, but the 200 rifles would change the whole complexion of the struggle and turn the Bogsiders into the aggressors. That in turn would lose us support. Besides, I hadn't a clue how many people in the Bogside knew how to use weapons. I myself couldn't load a rifle, never mind fire one, and I was sure that I was typical of the vast majority of the population. Only those who had served with the British army during the war would know anything about guns. Anyway, they would hardly have had the stomach for gunfights with the RUC or the British army. Keenan's promise that 'only sticks, stones and good old petrol bombs' would be used in the defence of the Bogside had swung a lot of people behind the Defence Association. The appearance of a large number of guns would undermine that support and we would lose the moral edge, which we had managed to maintain. Most importantly, if we resorted to armed resistance we would give the authorities a pretext for killing hundreds of people. Thanking the Donegal men for their concern, I politely declined their offer and the deputation left.

Letterkenny, twenty-one miles from Derry, was in Neil Blaney's constituency, and its people were magnificent hosts to the refugees from Derry who were streaming across the border. They brought stories of hungry people making a last stand in the Bogside against the forces of the Northern Ireland government. The stories lost nothing in the telling and gained something with each retelling. The Golden Grill, a restaurant owned by a senator, dispatched food, including two boxes of cooked chickens, to Derry. The chickens were left in my hallway. Johnny McDevitt, a close friend of Seán Keenan, had taken on the job of supplying the young defenders on the top of the flats with food. He came to my house shortly after the supplies arrived. He took the chickens to the flats, where the boys hoisted them up with a ball of twine. The boys, whose boyhood had ended, were tired and hungry after hours of defending the Bogside. With petrol-soaked hands they tore at the chicken. Halfway through 'Operation Chicken' the police launched an attack, advanced a hundred yards and came within striking distance of the stairway leading to the top of the flats. Busy with the chickens, and struggling to disperse the thick mist of CS gas around the entrances to the flats, McDevitt didn't notice the policemen until they were almost on top of him. Startled by the thump of heavy boots and realising the danger he was in, he looked around for stones with which to defend himself. Finding none, he resorted to bombarding the RUC men with cooked chickens – holding them off for the few vital moments that it took for reinforcements to arrive and drive the police back.

In a manoeuvre led by my third son, Declan, the rioters switched the action to Great James Street. This Georgian thoroughfare on the edge of the Bogside led up to the cathedral. Hearing sounds of fighting, people thought that the cathedral was about to be attacked. Only their dark uniforms and black helmets distinguished the policemen from a mass of loyalists confronting the Bogsiders outside the cathedral. The RUC made no visible effort to disperse these rioters, who seemed to revel in their immunity. The darkness of the night was illuminated by the continued explosions of petrol bombs flung by nationalists on the high ground surrounding the cathedral. They pushed a commandeered ice-cream van into position at the top of the hill. Petrol bombs exploded inside the service area. The crowd stood by expectantly as the brakes were released and the van began careering down the hill towards the RUC and their civilian auxiliaries. Inside the van, strawberry and vanilla ice cream melted in the heat from the burning petrol. The van swept down the hill, its PA blasting out Sandy Shaw's 'Puppet on a String':

I wonder if one day that you say that you care
If you say you love me madly, I'll gladly be there

Halfway down the steep street the van swerved, collided with a lamp-post and exploded, but Sandy Shaw sang on about love to the hate-filled city. As the battle raged around the cathedral, the ageing Bishop Farren paced from room to room, his anxiety rising by the minute. He went into a curate's room and sat down to compose himself. He immediately sprang up again and drew back the counterpane, to discover an air rifle.

Nothing could incense the Bogsiders as much as a perceived threat to their cathedral. They hastened towards it in their hundreds. A headmaster was spotted scurrying towards the cathedral, his furled umbrella dangling on his forearm. Hume borrowed a black beret at Number 10, armed himself with a cudgel and joined the rush towards St Eugene's.

It wasn't hard to distinguish the sharp crack of gunfire from the thud of the CS-gas guns. As the third gunshot casualty of the night was taken to hospital, the enthusiasm of the cathedral's defenders began to wane. Sticks, stones and good old petrol bombs were useless against superior weaponry. Foot by foot the police and their auxiliaries cleared the defenders from around the cathedral. The fact that they made no attempt to enter the church grounds was lost on the remains of the nationalist crowd, now being driven back into the Bogside and up towards Marlborough Terrace. By now they numbered no more than 150 and were almost exhausted. Hume and Keenan were among them. Hume half-heartedly bowled a stone in the direction of the police. It stopped well short of the police lines. It looked as if we had shot our bolt. It seemed only a matter of time before the police occupied the area. As Number 10 would doubtless be their first port of call, I had my family evacuated. My sons, who had grown to manhood and majored in Political Science during this long, hot summer, removed anything incriminating they could find from the house. Eileen was the last to leave. For the first time since I had built it eighteen years before, the house was empty and silent.

The barricades at the Little Diamond, Abbey Street and Rossville Street were only lightly defended but reports indicated that the police were simply holding the line beyond the barricades and were not making any effort to attack. Pat Clarke suggested a reconnoitre to establish their strength and disposition. It wasn't difficult to get behind the police lines. There were at least half a dozen exits from the Bogside through which people could pass unimpeded. Since 5 October 1968 the fighting had always been concentrated around William Street, the main entrance to the Bogside. Possession of that particular part of Derry seemed to be more important to both sides than the resolution of their differences. Clarke and I were amazed at the devastation visited upon Waterloo Square and William Street. We saw gutted shops and burnt-out buildings. Fire-brigade vehicles, with their long, snaking hoses, were damping down the guttering flames. It was impossible to walk without stepping on missiles such as half-bricks and cast-iron gratings. All the lights in William Street were out, adding to the sense of desolation. A food wagon was serving hot soup. From another vehicle someone was distributing canisters of CS gas to those policemen still standing. The wind must have changed, for their eyes were watering from the effects of the CS gas they had earlier fired into the Bogside. Policemen were lying around all over the place – some sleeping, but most too exhausted to sleep. Their tunics were open, their bootlaces loosened and their faces blackened with smoke. They had the vacant gazes of defeated men. 'Christ! They're hammered!' said Pat Clarke. 'There is no way they can take the Bogside tonight.' I remembered the VE Day parade in London in 1945. All the armed forces of the British Empire took part in the march. The men from Northern Ireland, with their black uniforms and the harp on their caps, all of them well over six feet tall, received a tremendous ovation. All around me I heard people ask, 'Who are they? Where do they come from?'

'They're Irish,' I had answered with pride.

As I gazed at the exhausted policemen who had allowed themselves to become stooges for the Unionist Party, I realised the contradiction in my own thinking. I was leading a revolt and yet respect for law and order was deeply ingrained in my character. And I knew that a society that didn't respect authority would go nowhere. But most of all, my hope of one day living in a united Ireland, where all citizens – Catholic, Protestant or whatever – enjoyed the same rights had faded away, like the morale of the exhausted men lying around me. A polite greeting from a senior police officer – 'Good night, Mr Doherty' – lent a surreal touch to the scene.

We hurried to Marlborough Terrace, where we insisted that what was left of the Catholic crowd should remain in the centre of the road to create the illusion of a mass of people. Help was on the way. The large housing estate on the hill overlooking the Bogside, Creggan, was another monument to gerrymandering. It had been built to keep the rising Catholic population within the boundaries of the South Ward. After a quarter of a century, it now had 14,000 inhabitants, many originally from the Bogside. Creggan had not seen any fighting, although many of its people had been at the barricades. Now it was time to get the rest involved. Doctor Donal MacDermott and Finbar O'Doherty roused the populace. They toured the streets by car with a loud hailer, calling for support for the defenders of the Bogside. The doctor wasn't having much success, so he handed the loud hailer to Finbar. His loud and lurid description of an attack on the cathedral by hordes of RUC men and loyalist extremists had a tone of urgency. Lights came on and people appeared in doorways. Finbar carried on, warming to his task. Hastily donning trousers and shoes, the men appeared and, in clutches, headed for the Bogside as dawn was breaking. By breakfast-time the tide had turned. Number 10 filled up again and the production of food restarted. Just as supplies were running out, a breadman emptied a vanload of bread onto the pavement. He didn't want payment.

CHAPTER 10

Neither Keenan nor I had slept since the early hours of Monday morning. It was now Thursday, but he showed no signs of fatigue. Always meticulous about his appearance, he washed and shaved at my place and prepared to face another day. I was in a state of near-collapse. The fighting had intensified and spread throughout nationalist areas of Northern Ireland. The government played the last card in its pack. The Minister of Home Affairs ordered the B-Specials to report for duty to Derry. With the mobilisation of the B-Specials, the tension in the Bogside heightened. We were both fearful and determined. We had wondered when they would be used against us and who would help us in the event of an armed attack. I felt a twinge of regret, recalling my refusal to accept the 200 rifles on offer from Donegal. I hoped I wouldn't live to rue my decision, although the rifles would only have allowed us to hold off an armed attack for a while.

It was incredible to watch the once-proud police force reeling under our continual attack. The defeat of the RUC was only a matter of hours away. But the B-Specials, still held in reserve, would be a different proposition. Once they had slipped the leash they would shoot to kill. Catholics feared and detested this special reserve force, which had been established by the Unionist oligarchs as a means of defending their supremacy and was recruited exclusively from the Protestant working class. Although the number of deaths directly attributable to them in the preceding fifty years was small, they had a reputation for ruthlessness. The shooting-up of a car carrying medical supplies for the Bogside seemed to confirm our worst fears. Our elation at having defeated the police was tempered by fear of attack by the 'Specials'. A number of members of the Defence Association retired to my house to discuss the situation. There weren't enough chairs for them in the front room of Number 10. Stanley Orme, the Labour MP, was sitting on the floor with his back to the wall. For years sympathetic to the cause of Irish unity, he had come to the Bogside as an observer. Suddenly from the street we heard shouts that soldiers were erecting barbed-wire barricades in Waterloo Square. I rushed outside. Dozens of people were milling around. Exposure to CS gas had made their eyes water and the tears streaked their smoke-blackened faces. What soldiers? Were they Irish or British? For one heart-stopping moment we thought that Lynch had lived up to his promise not to 'stand by'.

A Protestant crowd led by uniformed B-Specials had invaded Bishop Street and the burning of Catholic homes and businesses had begun in earnest. As I stood in the Bogside I could hear the sharp crack of breaking slates as the flames fought their way along the sloping roofs. I ordered Tommy Mellon to take some men with him to Bishop Street to try to contain the Protestant mob. Young Michael Feeney, who was in charge of fire-fighting, went with his squad to rescue anyone who was in danger from the fires. The only tools they had were axes, ropes and ladders.

I ran into the house again and asked Stanley Orme if he could phone London to check whether or not the troops would move against the people at the barricades. He replied: 'There is no way that a phone call to London, even to the Prime Minister, can help. The man in charge today is the commander of the troops on the ground. His instructions will be to restore public order and unless someone can get to him and negotiate, he may do it by force of arms.' Orme agreed to try anyway. He, Michael Canavan and I headed for the main barricade in William Street.

The history books record that when the British general,

Dowcra, erected the walls of Derry in 1604–9, he laid waste to the surrounding region in his search for building materials. The builders of the barricade now stretching across Rossville Street had scavenged adjacent building sites for materials and had strengthened their barrier with scaffolding poles, rubble and a miscellaneous collection of household furniture. The police had breached it on several occasions with their armoured vehicles but nothing less than a tank would have got through it now. The block of buildings beyond the barricade, enclosed by William Street, Little James Street and Sackville Street, was now ablaze and the police had abandoned the area. Determination and apprehension characterised the faces of the Bogside's defenders. Canavan and I needed to wring information and intelligence from them. All they could tell us was that the British army had taken over the city centre and that the B-Specials were armed and on the streets.

Wondering what the army would do, Canavan, Orme and I scaled the barricade in search of the commander. The heat from the blazing buildings was intense. The fires were now out of control; flames leapt through holes in the roofs and spilled out of vacant windows. On our third attempt, we found a way past the burning buildings. At Sackville Street, the unfamiliar sight of British troops stopped me dead in my tracks. Behind a barbed-wire entanglement across the wide street, they stood shoulder to shoulder with policemen, their khaki battledress contrasting with the black uniforms of the RUC. My heart missed a beat when I saw the rifles with their fixed bayonets pointed in our direction. I was relieved when a group of cameramen and Paul Grace, the former chief marshal of the Derry Citizens' Action Committee, joined us. Things were tense for a time. The soldiers and policemen, perhaps thinking that they were facing the vanguard of the rioters, appeared to be getting ready for action. Our group moved slowly towards the barbed wire, careful not to do anything to confuse them or give them an excuse for firing at us. After the tumult in the Bogside, the no man's land between us was strangely silent, until I used the loud hailer to ask to speak to a senior officer. Continuing to walk at a measured pace, watching the reaction of the assembled soldiers and policemen, I said a silent prayer and repeated my request. Momentarily, the ranks opened and a section of barbed wire was pulled aside. A police officer said, 'Follow me.'

The four of us, accompanied by two police officers, were taken to the RUC headquarters on the Strand Road. As we entered through the pedestrian gate, we saw the B-Specials running through the main gate with sub-machine guns and .303 rifles, as if emphasising the seriousness of the situation in Derry. The RUC, the British army and the B-Specials were now mobilised against the people of the Bogside. The B-Specials had answered the minister's call, rather hastily. Their tunics were open at the neck, and one wore the same kind of flat helmet as the bronze figure on the war memorial in the city centre.

Lieutenant Colonel Todd appeared small and insignificant in the presence of the hefty black-clad police officers. Todd wore no cap, and a few strands of his hair hung over his brow. He was informally dressed, with his battledress open at the neck, while the RUC men wore shiny, peaked caps and had their tunics buttoned up. The hand grenades strapped to Todd's chest showed that he was ready for action. The policeman who accompanied the senior RUC officer, Inspector Hood, said: 'We have been trying to get in touch with you people for two days.'

I ignored him and asked, 'Who's in charge here?'

'I am,' replied Todd.

I addressed him directly: 'You must take the police and the B-Specials off the streets.'

'I can't. I have only 150 men and another 150 on the way.

I need the police and the B-Specials to restore order,' Todd claimed.

'With them you will never restore order; without them half of the men you have will be enough,' I retorted.

Todd shook his head. Stanley Orme stepped forward and said: 'I am a Member of Parliament at Westminster. Listen to this man: it's your only hope of achieving peace. These people have suffered enough and will respond to any act of generosity.'

Todd turned to me and asked: 'Can you stop the fighting?"

'If you pull the police and the B-Specials out, we will cork the bottle on the other side,' was my reply.

Lieutenant Todd returned to Inspector Hood: 'Get your men off the streets.'

I shook hands with the British officer, then Canavan, Orme and I headed for the Bogside to keep our part of the bargain. Shortly afterwards, some of the defenders, led by Eddie McAteer, met a major at the bottom of William Street and asked for the withdrawal of the RUC. The officer complied and a cheer erupted from the crowd as the policemen and B-Specials marched back to barracks, leaving a lone British soldier to keep a peace which could not have been secured by an entire police force. I returned to the barricade in Rossville Street and, through the loud hailer, told the crowd that the fighting was over; that the RUC and B-Specials had gone back to their barracks and that the British army had assumed control. 'I have seen their weapons and have talked to their commanding officer. They will not, I repeat, will not attack if we stop fighting and remain behind our barricades. The RUC have been defeated,' I announced.

People felt a sense of relief. Most accepted the new reality, but not everyone was satisfied. As I moved off, I was accosted by a man reputed to be a local IRA officer. He blurted out: 'You bastard! You have let us down.'

'What do you mean?' I asked.

'We could have taken the army,' he shot back.

'We would have lost a thousand young boys,' I answered.

'They would have been expendable,' claimed Derry's answer to the armchair general in Dublin.

Nationalist Derry was relieved and proud yet indignant and apprehensive. The defeat of the police was sweet revenge for the killing of Sammy Devenny and for the raid on St Columb's Wells. More importantly, the government of Northern Ireland had cracked under the strain and had had to call for help. The British government had intervened in Derry. I recalled Michael Canavan's words after the London protest and asked him: 'Now that they are here, what can we do with them?' The exhausted young defenders temporarily suspended hostilities, overjoyed at their victory over the police. The people of the Bogside hoisted the warriors onto their shoulders and carried them through the streets. The shouts of the crowd echoed from the city walls. Men and women strained to touch the hands or slap the backs of the petrol-soaked boys, whom only a month before, during the riots of July, they had roundly condemned. Canavan said to me: 'I must get their names. We should never forget what they have done.' I watched the strong, well-dressed Canavan push through the milling crowd and thought about the incongruity of his presence here. He never talked about personal matters but it was generally believed that he had accumulated considerable wealth since taking over his father's business and that he had many other financial interests. He had a beautiful wife, a large family and a prestigious home. He enjoyed a high standing in the local business and professional community but had put this at risk by flirting with rebellion. Since Michael made the commitment to get involved in the agitation against the government at my daughter's wedding, the previous year, he had always been at the centre of things. But while others blew hot and cold and gave excuses for not being around in times of tension and danger, Michael had never faltered.

An uneasy peace settled over Derry. The British army stationed soldiers at strategic points along the perimeter of the area now surrounded by barricades. In a television interview I stated that 'The writ of the British queen no longer runs in Free Derry.' It was a Mexican stand-off.

Free Derry encompassed the Bogside, the sprawling Creggan housing estate, the more compact Brandywell and a small middle-class area. The territory held by the rebels roughly corresponded to the South Ward, which had been set up by the Unionist administration to contain the Catholic population of the city. The newly liberated territory measured 888 acres and two roods, or roughly one and a half square miles. By gerrymandering the city for over half a century, the Unionists had inadvertently created an Achilles heel for themselves. Twenty-eight thousand despised people shoved together, piled on top of each other and discriminated against, had decided that enough was enough. They were now outside the law, and their position, energy, and numbers posed a threat to the very existence of the state. In the vacuum created by the uneasy peace, we were playing a whole new game. From behind the barricades, which were now higher than ever, Free Derry proclaimed its independence to the world, and it appeared as if the whole world wanted to make our acquaintance. Congratulatory telegrams and letters flooded in. Telephones were few and far between in the Bogside, so many of the telephone messages were relayed by people in other parts of the city. The nearest telephone to me belonged to my neighbour, who was a foreman with the local Development Commission. The Defence Association desperately needed its own telephone. A GPO engineer came to install one. 'Black or green?' he asked.

'Green,' I said. Within minutes the telephone was working. He didn't give his name, or ask me to sign anything. He was only one of numerous government employees who performed many free services for us rebels.

During the fighting the Defence Association had exercised a modicum of control. It had replaced the Derry Citizens' Action Committee and had established its authority in Free Derry. With the exception of Bernadette Devlin's group, which operated out of Dermot McClenaghan's house in Wellington Street, it appeared that our authority enjoyed popular acceptance. The barricades were still intact, the British army had not fired a shot and no one – aside from Sammy Devenny – had been killed or seriously injured.

But anxiety soon replaced our euphoria. Following a discussion with Keenan, Canavan and I agreed to go to see the commander of the British forces. Barricades blocked the entrance to every street; burnt-out vehicles littered the place. Although two days had passed since the last rounds of CS gas had been pumped into the area, the stuff still clung to every pile of rubble and irritated my nostrils as Michael and I walked past the blackened hulks of buildings in William Street. There was no knowing what awaited us as we approached the RUC barracks. We had not formulated any plan. We were simply anxious to end the stalemate which had followed the Battle of the Bogside. Upon our arrival at the barracks, Canavan and I were taken immediately to the army's new headquarters at the rear of the complex. On our way through the barrack yard we passed dozens of policemen who were lounging about and desultorily kicking a football around. Their listlessness reminded me of the captured German soldiers I had seen in England after the invasion of Normandy. Defeat had sapped the Germans' vitality and they were now at the mercy of their new khaki-uniformed masters. As we shook hands with Lieutenants Colonel Todd and Millman, I was taken aback by their effusive greetings. 'We have been desperately trying to contact you since Thursday but couldn't. You have no phone, Mr Doherty.'

'Perhaps you could remedy that,' I replied, tongue-in-cheek.

'There's a long waiting list for phones. I can put a landline over the tops of the houses from our headquarters to your house,' the colonel said.

'I don't think that would be wise,' I replied, 'but the GPO might give the matter a priority rating if they were approached by the army.'

Lieutenant Colonel Millman wrote a note to remind himself to sort out the matter. Within a few days, the army had prevailed upon the GPO to provide me with a second telephone.

The British officers were anxious to regularise communications with Free Derry and tried to convince Canavan and me that the danger was now past and that the people could relax and take down the barricades. 'Certain conditions would have to be met before the barricades would come down,' said Canavan.

'What are those conditions?' asked Colonel Todd.

Canavan looked at me. Many demands had been promulgated since the start of the civil-rights campaign, but the colonel's question had taken us by surprise. Michael said he needed time to consult me, so we retired to the other end of the room. We hurriedly drew up and presented two lists to the British commander. These contained short-term and long-term demands. As we read them out, Lieutenant Colonel Millman wrote them down in longhand. When he had completed the document, he wrote out a copy, also in longhand. Asking Canavan and me to sign both, he gave one to me and said that the other would be presented to the Northern Ireland Cabinet as soon as possible. 'My God,' said Canavan as we left the building, 'you would think we had the backing of the Russian twelfth and fourteenth armies.'

When I returned home, I was told that Father O'Neill had called at the house and had been in a state of some agitation. He had gone to Nelson Street, where an angry crowd had gathered. I hurtled off to Nelson Street and met him there. He said, 'Bernadette heard that you and Canavan had gone to see the British military and called a public meeting. She has accused both of you of selling out and agreeing to have the barricades removed.' Outside the house which Bernadette was using as a headquarters was the burned-out carcass of a minibus. I scrambled on top of it and held aloft the copy of the document Canavan and I had signed in the presence of the British commander. I could see the apprehension on the faces of the people below me. They had been let down so often in the past that their expectations were always tainted with scepticism. I spoke, saying, 'There are those in the Bogside who are not of the Bogside but who would try to sow disunity among the people for their own selfish reasons. They have accused members of the Defence Association of treachery. I will read from the list of demands presented by the Defence Association to the British army.'

I slowly and deliberately read out the main points of our demands:

1   We have demanded the abolition of Stormont.
2   We have demanded the disbandment of the B-Specials.
3   We have demanded that all persons arrested during the fighting be released without charge.
4   No RUC or military personnel are to enter the Bogside or Creggan.
5   We remain at war with Stormont until these demands are met.

Signed: Michael Canavan and P. L. Doherty on behalf of the Derry Citizens' Defence Association.

Deliberately turning to face my accuser's house, I said: 'Does this look like you were sold out?' No sound came from the house.

'Get back to the barricades, strengthen them and prepare to defend them against any attackers,' was my final comment.

The peace had been saved – just about. The British army was now in control and was strong enough to storm our barricades. The RUC had in effect been stood down; it had failed to maintain law and order. The British army had intervened at the request of the Northern Ireland government. It had come to re-establish law and order on behalf of the civil power. The Bogsiders had neatly usurped the army's role. Order had been restored and we had kept our side of the bargain, but the authorities were now faced with a community inside the United Kingdom which refused to accept any authority outside itself. The soldiers were cooling their heels on the edge of a rebellious but apparently peaceful community. How peaceful that community would remain depended on the commander of the British forces.

John Bradley had been a Justice of the Peace for a number of years and was a member of the Northern Irish judiciary. He had agonised long and hard over whether to accept his appointment as a JP. He passionately believed in Irish unity and hadn't much time for the northern statelet or its institutions. He discussed the matter with me and we agreed that the help he would be in a position to offer his own community was more important than his own political views. His appointment would mean that people could get a sympathetic hearing from, and be served by, a man of outstanding ability and integrity who was one of their own. Everyone knew where Bradley stood politically. He had little respect for the state but was prepared to use his talents within the system for the benefit of his own people. I asked him to take a deputation of Catholic JPs to Colonel Todd in order to convince him that he was not dealing with a ragamuffin gang of dissidents but with a sorely tried and angry people. A surprised Colonel Todd received these ultra-respectable citizens at his headquarters. This group of servants of the state declared their support for the Bogsiders. It was a calculated move to counter the loyalist demands that the army bring down the barricades and subdue the rebels. And it worked.

Many Protestants believed that the rioting had been directed by the IRA, and they were fearful and angry. Peter Pan did nothing to allay their fears. From the safety of his builder's yard, he announced that he was sending his paper battalions north to defend the Catholic population. His nonsensical threat destroyed any residual belief Keenan and I still had in him.

I built upon the delegation's success by persuading Michael Canavan to invite some officers to his home. Canavan's neighbours in comfortable Talbot Park watched an advance party of soldiers drive up in jeeps, followed by Colonel Millman and Major Mike Reynolds. A dozen soldiers, their rifles at the ready, surrounded the house. His neighbours knew about Canavan's involvement in the civil-rights movement and must have thought that the soldiers had come to whisk him off to jail. The soldiers were ready for anything, the officers stiff and wary, but a few large whiskies and some friendly banter soon eased the tension. In less than an hour the army had withdrawn without losing a man. Canavan and I burst into uncontrollable laughter as the last jeep disappeared up the road. If the visit of the Catholic JPs hadn't totally dispelled the idea that we were all commie good-for-nothings, then Canavan's gracious welcome and bounteous hospitality definitely had.

Having established the authority of the Defence Association in Free Derry, I headed to the parochial house to see Bishop Farren. He received me warmly and expressed his appreciation of the visit. 'It is seventeen years since anyone in public life has come to visit me.' This surprised me, as it was generally felt that he exercised control over the Catholics of his diocese through a group of influential middle men. I asked for his support for the Defence Association. On Sunday his statement was read from the altar at every Mass in the city.

Later on, he was to cause quite a stir when he paid a return visit to the headquarters of the Defence Association. He brought with him the Indian Bishop of Agra. All the neighbours flocked to the house. He was introduced to Father Twohig from Cork who was acting as an unofficial chaplain to the Defence Association. A few days later, Father Twohig, who was apparently on sick leave, was called back to Cork.

CHAPTER 11

The voice was unmistakably southern Irish, slightly nasal but with an air of authority. 'Charles Haughey speaking. Can I have a word with Paddy Doherty?' I identified myself. After some pleasantries, Haughey got down to business: 'You'll need some money up there. How much do you need?' I couldn't believe it: the Irish Minister for Finance was offering me money over a phone line which the authorities must have been tapping. It didn't seem to concern him that someone might be listening in, or that his offer might become public knowledge. My spirits soared as the full implications of Haughey's offer sank in. After the Taoiseach's promise not to stand by, an Irish minister was offering to bankroll the Defence Association. To me, the minister's apparent lack of concern for secrecy indicated a commitment on the part of the government, something which was more important to me than money. It represented a historic and direct intervention in the internal affairs of Northern Ireland by the Republic. Our original defence fund of eighty-seven pounds had been spent, as the half a million pounds' worth of burnt-out buildings around me attested. In the momentum of the fighting and the euphoria of victory we had lost our sense of the value of money. As I hesitated, Haughey said, 'I'll send you five thousand.'

'No,' I replied, 'one thousand would be plenty. Any more could prove to be an embarrassment.' Next day a banker came to my door to tell me that a sum of money had been deposited and that the bank awaited instructions for the management of the account. I contacted Michael Canavan, who asked Tommy Carlin, a director in Derry Credit Union, to set up a book-keeping system for the Defence Association. The two men's ability, integrity and financial experience eased what would have been an onerous burden on Keenan and me. Soon we received another thousand pounds. We agreed to forward this money to the bishop, who was overwhelmed with requests for assistance.

The Defence Association produced a daily news-sheet which was printed on one or other of the Roneo printing machines in use in local schools. Once, when nothing else was available, we used the parish printing press in the parochial house at St Eugene's. Peter Tarleton, a young Church of Ireland clerical student, was the main news writer, and his careful wording often concealed deep disagreements within the Defence Association. Eamonn McCann welded the left-wing Republicans and the Young Socialists into a cohesive force within the association. He always held a meeting of his faction every night before the regular meeting of the main group. The only declared Republicans he didn't try to recruit were Keenan, Neil Gillespie and Tommy Mellon, whom he regarded as past it and unimportant. McCann had a block of eleven out of a total of forty-four members. There was no clearly defined opposition to him. On any night when the attendance dropped below 50 per cent, or on an average night, when thirty people were in attendance, McCann had a good chance of having his motions approved. He contested each and every democratic decision taken by the Defence Association with which he disagreed. He did so by calling impromptu public meetings or by using his own news-sheet, *Barricade Bulletin*, to present his own point of view. I was the main target of the McCannites. They consistently opposed my opinions. I knew from my sources who were attending McCann's meetings and I was able to confuse his supporters by proposing motions with which I secretly disagreed. Their frustration at this tactic was expressed most forcefully by a left-wing Republican who declared: 'You bastard. I don't know whether to vote for you or against you because I never know whether you want your own motion carried or defeated.'

'It might help if you voted on the merits of the case instead of reacting to the pull of a string,' I responded, with equal vehemence.

The Defence Association established itself as the only group entitled to speak for the people behind the barricades and I became its spokesman. My continuing absence from my job was causing my employer some concern. It was becoming increasingly unlikely that I would return to work in the short term, so I decided to let my employers know that I was taking extended leave, to allow them to find someone to replace me. Mary Holland agreed to take me to Gerald Black's house on the Culmore Road. Black was a senior partner in John Eakin and Company, the firm with which I had spent the greater part of my working life.

It was a beautiful summer evening. Black's roses had passed their best but the garden was a riot of colour and a tonic for the eyes after the smoke-blackened Bogside. As I walked up the driveway, Black, who was plucking the faded petals from his roses, turned on hearing the footsteps on the tarmac. 'You are having big times,' my boss said. 'What is it you are after?' He had served as a captain in the British army during the Second World War and from his tone I had no doubt that my recent activities had upset him.

My reply was to the point: 'We intend to finish Stormont for all time.'

'I suppose you'll want your united Ireland after that?' Another rose petal floated to the ground.

'Why not?' I responded uncompromisingly. It was the only time we had discussed politics in all the years we had worked together.

Gerald Black turned to his roses once again, and I walked back down the drive and out of the job which had sustained my family for more than twenty years.

The police identified the five men who had tried to burn down the RUC station in Rosemount. Rather than drop the matter – after all, Hume's truce had saved their station – the graceless RUC charged the men and summoned them to appear in court. A District Inspector was given the task of presenting the case for the prosecution of the five. The DI had a lean, handsome face; a slight hook at the end of his nose gave him a hawkish appearance. Michael Canavan and I both knew of his reputation as a tough but fair policeman who kept his own men in line. Our interview with him lasted over an hour, and during it we discussed the possibility of renewed violence and the general political situation. Michael Canavan inquired whether any of the Protestant civilians who had attacked the Bogside with the police had been charged. 'They haven't,' the DI replied.

'If the men who attacked the police station pleaded guilty, what would happen?' Michael enquired. 'That is a matter for the court,' the officer answered. Canavan spoke softly and menacingly. He asked a series of questions, each time receiving non-committal answers. Not once did he suggest striking a bargain. Instead he reiterated that if the police and the courts took a hard line, there could be a reaction on the streets. It was a difficult interview. Both sides stood their ground. Canavan and I decided to ask the men to plead guilty. On Monday morning the court was packed with relatives of the men and a large number of policemen. The charges were read out and I held my breath as the DI rose to his feet: 'I have nothing to add, your honour,' he said. There were angry murmurs from the contingent of policemen in the courtroom. 'Fifty pounds each,' declared the magistrate. The friends and relations of the accused cheered. Canavan paid the fines and I gave a sigh of relief.

McCann and his camarilla seemed to forget that others besides them had been fighting to defend the Bogside. McCann, Bernadette Devlin and Louden Seth, an English political activist and friend of theirs, turned up at my door one day. They were in a buoyant, self-assured mood. They joined the discussion going on in the front room. Hume and Cooper had arrived earlier and I quickly sensed the animosity between my two sets of guests. I remained silent as they launched into merciless criticism of each other. No one seemed to realise that the Defence Association was the ultimate authority now. The politicians had failed; Bernadette and her friends, despite their valuable contribution, were outsiders. Cooper accused Bernadette of using the situation to build up her own image. She in turn accused him of jealousy. It was spiteful, acrimonious stuff. I broke in: 'Regardless of what has happened or who was in charge up until now, I want to make it clear that the Defence Association is the only authority within the Bogside. It will issue all instructions for the defence or organisation of the area and we will expect these instructions to be obeyed.'

McCann was the first to react, contesting the validity of my statement. I no longer had any doubts about where he was coming from. Turning to him, I said: 'We are in a very dangerous situation. If you attempt to use it to your own political advantage, some people may be killed.' I paused, and then continued: 'If this happens I personally will kill you.' I held his gaze until he lowered his eyes. Turning to Bernadette, I said: 'Your contribution has been important, but you don't belong here.'

Louden Seth, who was sitting on the floor, made to defend his friends and attempted to get to his feet. 'If you get off that floor, I will throw you out the window behind you,' I told him. He returned to his position on the floor. I had directly and brutally asserted my authority. McCann remained silent. He knew I meant business. Bernadette began sobbing uncontrollably. During the confrontation, Hume and Cooper left. Eileen consoled Bernadette and took her upstairs to a bedroom to rest. I waited until Bernadette had recovered before visiting her. She was depressed and deeply concerned for the people of Northern Ireland. 'There is no light at the end of the tunnel; they will be destroyed,' she said. She had shouldered the lonely burden of leadership and it was crushing her. I tried to reassure her, telling her that others were able and willing to share the load.

A few days later, Bernadette took up a long-standing invitation to visit America, and left the Bogside. Soon we heard that she had upset Irish America. She was a wonderful orator but her political thinking was anathema to the emigrant community. She threw in her lot with minority groups, whatever their political aspirations, and championed the Black Panthers, a radical black organisation which terrified Middle America. Her final insult was to hand the key to the city of New York to the Panthers, after she had received it with all the pomp and circumstance the city's Irish community could manage. Most Irish Americans were fanatically anti-British but politically conservative. Bernadette exposed a contradiction in their attitudes: they demanded civil rights for the people of Northern Ireland but were less keen on civil rights for black Americans. Her visit was important in another way. For the first time in many years Irish-Americans had been reaching into their wallets to help the people of Northern Ireland. When Bernadette summoned up the spectres of revolutionary socialism and the brotherhood of man they returned their wallets to their hip pockets.

Colonel Todd, who had accepted my offer of a truce, bid farewell to Derry, and Brigadier Leng took command of the west of Northern Ireland. I soon built up a good relationship with the new commander. 'Jobs are what you need around here,' he said. 'We have got to get jobs for the young people.' There was no doubting the well-bred soldier's sincerity, or his concern for the people whom he believed history had thrust into his care. He saw himself as an instrument for peace and reconciliation and expressed the belief that extremists, in any situation, would eventually bury their differences and unite to fight the establishment. He illustrated his theory for me by referring to the hands of a clock: 'The further the hands get away from twelve o'clock, the closer they get to being together at six.' His belief that Republicans and loyalists would come together to destroy the established order indicated to me how little he understood the Irish question. With great sincerity he argued that 'the government must find work for young Catholic men' in order to prevent our slide into anarchy.

Colonel Millman didn't have Brigadier Leng's cut-glass accent or suave manner. Professionalism rather than poise had taken him up through the ranks. He didn't have the brigadier's simplistic approach to Irish politics either. He was prepared to wheel and deal with the people behind the barricades and made himself available night and day for negotiations. He always pronounced my name with a 'c'. 'Mr Docherty, the bus being used as a barricade in Rosemount is a very new and very expensive vehicle. Could the bus company have it back, please?' he pleaded.

'That bus was captured during hostilities with the police and is now part of our defence system. We won't be returning that bus until we see the response from the government to our demands,' I explained.

There was a short silence on the line. 'If your people are worried about an attack by Protestant extremists, the army will supply barricade material if you will return the bus.'

I wasn't quite sure I had heard him correctly. I asked him to repeat what he had just said. I received another bizarre reply. 'The army will supply the people with enough timber and barbed wire to erect a substantial barricade, if the bus now being used as a barricade is returned.'

This time I fell silent, thinking of the propaganda we could generate from this swap. His offer was more than reasonable. The Defence Association couldn't lose, but I didn't have the right to make a decision off my own bat. 'Colonel, the people of Rosemount captured that bus and only they have the power to release it. I'll put your request before the committee tonight.'

The Defence Association considered the matter that evening and agreed it was a matter for the Rosemount Area Committee. I was appointed to go to talk with them. The meeting took place in the girls' school in the 'village', as Rosemount was called, and was conducted in a most competent and democratic fashion. The army's request to have the bus returned was solemnly discussed. I had expected some ideological opposition but the canny 'villagers' presented a pragmatic, practical argument against returning the bus. It completely closed off the street and, more importantly, provided cover for people on barricade duty during the long, cold nights. The committee felt that while the army's offer to provide barricade material was laudable and would meet their defence requirements, the comfort of the vigilantes on duty could not be prejudiced. Request denied. I believed the Defence Association had missed an excellent photo-opportunity but I had to bow to the authority of the Rosemount Committee.

Early next morning I was at headquarters with Michael Canavan when Colonel Millman phoned again. 'Mr Docherty, what about the bus?' Millman asked. 'I'm sorry, Colonel, the Rosemount people rejected your offer,' I answered.

We discussed the cost of the bus and the possibility of it being damaged or even burned. Then Michael Canavan, sitting beside me, made a brilliant suggestion: 'Tell him that the people might accept an old bus to replace the new one.'

The colonel promised to phone back within two hours. He must have had a difficult job selling the idea to the bus company because almost four hours had gone by before he called again. 'The bus company have agreed to supply an old bus if the one in the barricade is released. How soon can we make the switch?' he asked.

I knew I had to persuade the Rosemount Committee to agree and I needed time to tip off the reporters. I wanted to milk the opportunity for all it was worth. 'Tomorrow morning at ten o'clock,' I replied.

Canavan, myself and the whole 'village' turned out the following morning, accompanied by a gaggle of reporters and photographers. On the stroke of ten, under army escort, a company driver brought the obsolete bus into Rosemount. The driver inflated the tyres of the barricade-bus and installed a battery. The first turn of the switch brought life to the engine and cheers from the crowd. No damage had been done to the bus and the 'villagers' were justifiably proud. As the soldiers started to manoeuvre the replacement bus into position to reconstruct the barricade, I returned to headquarters. It was an amazing coup for the Rosemount people. There was a festive air about the place as I left.

Within half an hour I was summoned back to Rosemount, where an angry crowd of citizens had surrounded a jeep and were refusing to release the driver and passengers. The army were preparing to rescue them. Things were looking pretty ugly. I wondered what had happened. Phil O'Donnell explained: the bus released was a forty-four-seater and the replacement was a thirty-two-seater. When in position it was six feet too short to close off the entrance to the street. Feeling short-changed, the angry residents were demanding that the army let them use the jeep to plug the gap. After negotiations, the army agreed to supply sufficient timber and barbed wire to close off the street. The jeep, its driver and passengers were then released.

The Defence Association's news-sheet for 28 August announced that 'Seamus O'Callaghan will visit the area at 3 pm today.' The tongue-in-cheek Gaelicisation of the name of the British Home Secretary, whose forbears hailed from Cork, also reflected our hope that he might have some sympathy with Irish nationalism. As a general rule, Callaghan's Labour Party was more sympathetic to the minority in Northern Ireland. Labour MPs had marched on 5 October in Duke Street. The announcement didn't advert to an acrimonious debate the night before, or to the frenzied preparations for the arrival of the man who was ultimately responsible for law and order in Northern Ireland. Colonel Millman was insisting that the army had a duty to accompany and protect the Home Secretary during his visit behind the barricades. We told him in no uncertain terms that the Defence Association would take responsibility for Callaghan's safety and that he would be protected by our security force.

Millman was in a spot. Unless he relinquished his responsibility for the safety of the Home Secretary and handed him over to the rebels behind the barricades, Callaghan would not be allowed into a part of the UK over which neither the army nor the police exercised any authority. Millman reluctantly gave in. We removed all unnecessary barricades and cleared the streets of rubble. I ordered that the gable in St Columb's Wells bearing the slogan, 'You are now entering Free Derry' be painted white, with the lettering in black capitals. The painter only charged for materials. Seeing the bold, professional inscription, some complained that I had 'institutionalised' the voice of the people.

As far as I was concerned, 'Big Vinny' Coyle was the voice of the people. The two-hundred-and-fifty-pound former civil-rights marshal and 'electioneer' for Hume had been one of the main men during the long months of agitation. He was an imposing figure, standing tall under a large, wide-brimmed hat. His colourful language had got us out of many scrapes and he clearly loved being at the centre of the action. Prior to his Bogside engagement, Callaghan met the Londonderry Development Commission, which had been in control of the city since Terence O'Neill had done away with the unlamented Londonderry Corporation. Timing it brilliantly, 'Big Vinny' met Callaghan and his escorts as they left the Guildhall, and walked the short distance to the main barricade with them. As Hume, Keenan and I stepped forward to greet the Home Secretary, Vinny introduced Hume with the words, 'Jim, meet my friend, John Hume.'

Callaghan's reception reflected the confusion in our colonised minds. Thousands turned out filled with hope and expectation to welcome him. He was presented with flowers and people surged forward from the crowd, hands outstretched, to touch him. One woman kissed his hand. Among us there persisted the illusion that British politicians were potential allies. They were unaware of conditions in Derry, but if we enlightened them – so the thinking went – they would do something to help us. Keenan and I, the Defence Association appointees, and Hume, the MP for the area, formed the reception committee. Our job was to greet Callaghan and escort him to a meeting with the leaders of the Defence Association, who were waiting in the Bogside Inn. The three of us represented different strands within the nationalist community: Keenan, the Republican, with his belief in armed struggle; Hume, the constitutionalist; and me, the pragmatic wheeler-dealer. It said a lot for Keenan's integrity that he carried out the Defence Association's instructions, despite his utter lack of faith in British politicians.

Our handshakes with Callaghan were the signal for our security corps to relieve the British soldiers of responsibility for ensuring Callaghan's safety. The soldiers, with their loaded rifles, moved away and Bogsiders wearing white armbands surrounded Callaghan. Tommy Carlin, the namesake of the man appointed to look after the financial affairs of the Defence Association, pushed forward, holding a faded photograph. It showed a Labour delegation which had visited trade unionists in Derry fifteen years earlier. They had expressed concern for the unemployed. A young, lean Callaghan and Carlin himself were visible in the photograph. 'This was taken in 1954. I was unemployed then, and I have been unemployed since. You were the devil then and you are still the devil,' Carlin hissed. The incident highlighted the despair and sense of betrayal felt by the unemployed in Derry. Callaghan was visibly rattled but said nothing. He mightn't have made himself heard, anyway, over the bustle and excitement in the street.

Carlin was not the only one opposed to Callaghan's visit. The groups who disagreed with the Defence Association now swung into action. Their ferocity made up for their weakness in numbers. Their members hoisted placards and made a few attempts to break the security ring. Most people tried to isolate the protesters, but as they crowded around the official party, they made movement towards the meeting-place impossible.

Callaghan's bodyguards – four plain-clothes policemen – proved powerless as the crowd surged up William Street, sweeping Callaghan and the reception committee along with it. I had to admire his courage, for he was now at the mercy of a people who had humbled a police force only days earlier. British soldiers were cooling their heels on the edge of the Bogside and the lone army helicopter high up in the sky could offer no help. It was hard to stay on our feet. Once or twice I feared for Callaghan's safety. I knew that no one would deliberately injure him, but if he had fallen he might have been trampled underfoot. Finally we broke out and entered the house of a Mrs Diver on the Lecky Road, about a hundred yards from where the Defence Association sat awaiting Callaghan's arrival.

Almost exhausted and nervously mopping his brow, Callaghan slumped into the small, upholstered settee. I sent word to the committee members that the venue of the meeting had been changed. With typical obstinacy, a number refused to attend and demanded that the original venue remain. Eamonn McCann, whom I suspected had organised the opposition to Callaghan, joined the group in the small house, and negotiations began. During the meeting, other members of the Defence Association arrived and sat down on the floor in the tiny room.

We described the injustices the Catholic people of Northern Ireland had suffered. We spoke to Callaghan as if he were a visitor from another planet, not the master of the circus at Stormont. He had been closely following recent events. He had given Chichester Clarke the green light to allow the 12 August march to proceed. He had also sanctioned the use of CS gas during the Battle of the Bogside. Canavan and McCann enumerated our long list of grievances. Callaghan nodded patronisingly. 'I can bind Stormont to ensure that discrimination can never again take place. I will change it and build into it the machinery which will protect your people,' he said. He chided the Defence Association for not appreciating the extent of its own success: 'I am here in the Bogside discussing with you the future of this country.' He explained that there were only two options open to the Catholics of Northern Ireland: we could continue with the agitation, which would provoke hardline loyalists into reacting and lead to more anarchy, bloodshed, burnings and terror; on the other hand, we could give him time to change the structures of Stormont.

Michael Canavan offered a third option: the abolition of Stormont. Callaghan replied, 'I can change the structure and even the ownership of Stormont, but I can't take down the sign. The loyalists will never tolerate the ending of Stormont.' He was facing both ways: he had to promise Catholics reforms while assuring Protestants of his continuing support for Stormont. It was complex; he appeared sincere, and I weakened.

Keenan said little, obviously convinced by now that negotiations were futile, and finding Callaghan's attitude condescending. Callaghan promised to come back to Northern Ireland to create the structures of a just society. The clamour outside was growing.

People were demanding to see and hear Callaghan. Using a loud hailer, the Home Secretary addressed the crowd, his ample form protruding through the half-opened window on the first floor. 'Some say I should be neutral. I am not neutral. I am on the side of right.' The crowd cheered. Keenan looked away. Callaghan returned to the street and the security corps hurried him by the shortest possible route to Protestant Fountain Street, where he received a muted but not hostile welcome.

CHAPTER 12

The barricades were perhaps the most evocative feature of Free Derry. They called to mind the French Revolution, the Paris Commune and other times when the common people had confronted the established order. The barricades were essential for our defence. Streets competed to build the best barricade. The children emulated their elders and competed among themselves to build the best mini-barricade. It was impossible to walk more than twenty yards without having to negotiate a pile of rubble topped with old household furniture. The delivery of essential services was becoming impossible.

Eugene O'Hare came to see me, accompanied by the chief engineer of the Londonderry Commission, a former colonel called McKinder. O'Hare was a chemist and had been Neil Gillespie's chess partner on the bridge during the march on 16 November. His composure might have had something to do with his long association with the game. I remembered him from school. Even as a boy he had been big and heavy. I had a vision of him with a hurley in his hand, the sweat streaming down his face as he chased a small leather orb around the playing fields in Brooke Park. He had joined the Nationalist Party and had been elected as a councillor. Years earlier, Father Mulvey had applied for planning permission to build houses for the homeless in the Pennyburn district, which had been designated an industrial area in the Area Plan. His plan was turned down by the corporation, forcing him to build on the side of a windswept hill within sight of Grianan of Aileach. Father Mulvey's perception was that those Nationalist councillors who voted with the Unionists did so to the detriment of the Catholic homeless of the city. I was surprised to see the two of them at my door. But the engineer merely wanted to know how he could help. Roads had to be cleared and refuse collected. How could these things be done? I remembered how many times people had talked about the possibility of total anarchy if our agitation went too far. We had certainly gone a long way, and now the institutions run by the McKinders of this world were adjusting to new realities. Institutions, I realised, knew how to preserve themselves. McKinder was anxious to get on with some building work. We discussed a proposed road-widening for Rossville Street, and the transportation of schoolchildren within the area. Some of the barricades were impeding his plans. McKinder promised to come back and agree work schedules with me; the other arms of the state would make similar arrangements. Individual servants of these institutions refused to cooperate with us, but most continued to serve an area where the queen's writ no longer ran.

On Sunday 31 August, I requested the removal of some of the external barricades. For three hours the Defence Association discussed my proposal. Would it be a sign of weakness? Would it be a betrayal of the people of Belfast? How many jobs would the building work create? The association was split but voted for the removal of three barricades in order to allow buses to pass through and the road-widening to proceed. The main barricade in Rossville Street was the most contentious. We voted to remove it and to replace it with moveable barbed-wire barriers. McCann's group were furious. I was ordered to implement the decision.

A group of European students – a kind of International Brigade – had taken up residence in the old West End Hall. They supported the minority faction on the committee. No sooner had I taken it down than they rebuilt the main barricade higher than before. The students had arrived after the Battle of the Bogside and had not seen any action. Their presence added a bit of colour to the Bogside but few of us took them seriously. By re-erecting the barricade they were overstepping the mark and deliberately undermining the authority of the Defence Association. A tall, blonde German shouted gutturally at me: 'You do not speak for the people of the Bogside! *I* do!'

'I damn well do,' I retorted. I watched the angry foreigners fussing around their rising barricade. I would need help to get it – and them – out of my hair. I had a short meeting with the dockers in the ATGWU hall. I explained my difficulty and asked them for support. 'Just name the time and place,' they answered. A large crowd gathered at the barricade, expecting a showdown. I had instructed the foreigners to remove the barricade by eight o'clock or else we would remove it ourselves. They defiantly sat down on top of the barricade and waited. At exactly eight o'clock I gave the order and the dockers moved in. Within an hour the road had been cleared and the authority of the Defence Association re-established. Later that night I was at a meeting during which a student shouted, 'Hitler used the dockers; Mussolini used the dockers; and now Doherty has used the dockers!'

It had been a close-run thing and it was some time before I raised the subject of barricades again. When I did, it was in peculiar circumstances. A car had been damaged at a barricade and its owner had submitted a claim for compensation to the Defence Association. I chose to ignore the claim but it came up at a meeting of the association. Where did responsibility lie and who was liable for the damages? Barricades were an emotive subject and it proved difficult for the association – a growing, democratic body – to arrive at a decision. The debate grew intense. All the old arguments were rehashed. Did we really need the barricades? What purpose were they serving? Was an attack possible? If we removed them, would we be betraying the people of Belfast? The debate went on for nearly four hours. It was after midnight when Frank Doran settled the issue: 'I hate the barricades; they represent fear and a fearful people cowering behind them. We have defeated a police force and brought a government to its knees, and we should be proud of our achievements, not cowering behind barricades. All we need is something tangible to indicate the territory of Free Derry.'

At this point I intervened to suggest that a simple white line, two inches in width, could mark off the area where the queen's writ did not run. It was as if the scales had fallen from everyone's eyes at the same time. Everybody was in agreement and we laughed at the audacity of the decision. At eight o'clock the next morning, a hired excavator and dump-trucks arrived to start removing the barricades. We had paint and brushes, and as soon as the road was swept clean, we began marking out the borders of Free Derry. This took up most of the day. Bemused British soldiers stood watching us, their weapons at the ready. I marked out the north side, then handed over the work to McCann.

Later that day I was called in to settle a dispute between the people of the Long Tower and the British army. McCann had painted the white line across the wrong end of a street, leaving about six houses outside Free Derry. To make matters worse, soldiers had shown up and erected a barbed-wire entanglement on McCann's white line. A group of angry residents were demanding that the army move the barbed wire to the other end of the street. My explanation for the mistake did not prove acceptable to the officer in charge. Things were getting tense. I rushed to the nearest phone and spoke to the staff major. He instructed me to order the officer in charge to move the barbed wire. The officer listened impassively as I relayed the new order.

Without saying a word, he walked off, soon returning to say that Colonel Millman had reversed the major's decision and that the barbed wire was to remain in its original position. By this time, more than a hundred angry people had surrounded the soldiers and an ugly confrontation was developing. I was now the target of the crowd's anger. I excused myself and this time phoned the brigadier general, who shouted down the phone: 'Tell the damn fool to move it immediately and tell him these are my orders.'

The poor officer couldn't believe his ears. He ran to his phone to check out the orders. In less than five minutes he was back and sheepishly offered to erect another barbed-wire entanglement on the spot which I had suggested. Exactly one hour later he would remove the first boundary. This pantomime was going on in front of a crowd that was growing larger and angrier by the minute. A second barbed-wire entanglement was built, enclosing the six houses and over a hundred people. For a solid hour I stood with the officer, confronting the crowd. Bang on time, watch in hand, he gave the order to dismantle the first entanglement. He had saved his honour; I had sweated blood during my lesson on the correct delineation of boundaries.

That was not the end of the matter. Unknown to us, the army had also discussed the barricades and had decided that while the barricades around the Free Derry area remained, it would only have to watch the three exits controlled by our own security people. The removal of the barricades forced them to rethink their plans. They had to send for reinforcements when the barricades came down and soldiers had to stand on every street to monitor traffic and pedestrians crossing the white line, without having the authority to pursue any vehicle or persons into Free Derry. A car had to be at least a metre outside the line before the soldiers could search the boot. Drivers would hear strange requests such as, 'Excuse me, sir, could you move forward a little so that I can examine the boot, because the rear of the car is over the white line and I am forbidden to step over it.' One exasperated officer jumped over the white line and jumped back again, shouting, 'Go tell Paddy Doherty that I was in Free Derry without his permission.'

In all this time, I didn't sleep much and seldom went to bed. Instead I catnapped in the armchair beside the telephone during the long hours of the night. No one else appeared to go to bed either. The people were on a permanent high, dashing here and there in cars, organising the policing of the area, sorting out family rows, taking people to hospital, closing pubs that were open after their allotted closing-time and keeping an eye out for strangers – tasks which have to be performed if a community under siege is to survive.

One night the door opened. One of the young men on security patrol entered, and stood to attention. 'I have captured two spies,' he said.

'Where?' I asked.

'On the Lone Moor Road in a car,' was his reply.

'Bring them in,' I ordered.

I was surprised to see a couple in their early twenties enter the room. I turned to the security guard and asked, 'What were they doing?'

'Sitting talking in a car,' was his sharp reply.

I asked the guard to leave and asked the young man whether he lived in the area. 'No, but I was leaving her home from a dance,' he said, pointing to the girl.

I felt embarrassed, but I suggested to them that courting at 3am in Free Derry was an extremely risky business. I dismissed them and thanked the youth for his vigilance. I was sorry that I did, because between 3am and dawn, no less than six courting couples were arrested by the same man and brought before me. Free Derry was a tough place for lovers.

The girl was about nineteen and her story was a common one in the Bogside. A court had ordered her brother to pay a fine. Many young people had been in court for rioting but he had broken into a local shop and had vandalised some stock. This had happened before the barricades went up and before Free Derry had been declared independent. She explained to me that her brother had been offered a job outside Free Derry but because the fine of nineteen pounds remained unpaid, he couldn't take the job. He was in a bind. As there was no money in the house, he needed the job to pay the fine, but because he hadn't paid the fine, he would be arrested and jailed before he could earn the money to pay it. I didn't have any money to help him. During my interview with the girl, I discovered that Louis McCafferty was the grocer whose shop had been vandalised. I went to see him. He was cutting rashers of bacon and acknowledged me with a nod. Wrapping the rashers up and finishing with his customer, he turned to me: 'Well, Paddy, what can I do for you?'

'Did you have your shop broken into some time ago?' I asked.

'I did,' he replied. 'It wasn't what was stolen that annoyed me, it was the sheer vandalism of it. Butter tramped into the ground, tea and sugar opened. What a mess!'

'Did you know the young lad who did it was fined nineteen pounds?' I probed.

'He should have got jail,' said McCafferty angrily.

The door opened and a customer entered. 'A pound of butter and two loaves,' she said. McCafferty's anger subsided as he dealt with his customer.

I resumed the conversation as she left the shop. 'The lad has got the offer of a job,' I said.

'I couldn't care less,' replied the grocer. 'What has that got to do with me?'

'He can't take the job because he hasn't paid the fine.'

'I've told you, he robbed me, wrecked my shop, destroyed my stock and if I had my way, it's jail he should have got,' he quickly retorted.

My tone was conciliatory. 'He's very young and he should be

given a chance. It also gives you an opportunity as well,' I added.

'What the hell do you mean? An opportunity to do what?' McCafferty scoffed.

'Pay his fine,' I said.

The grocer stopped stacking his shelves to respond to this incredible suggestion. 'Like hell I will. Pay the fine of the person who robbed me,' he muttered. 'If I was stupid or soft enough to do that, they wouldn't leave me with a pound of sugar on these shelves,' he continued.

I was glad to be interrupted for a second time. Nearly ten minutes went by before the customer left the shop. I stood there looking at McCafferty, who grew more and more uncomfortable, struggling with his conscience while attending to the customer. Finally he said: 'If I pay it, will you tell no one?'

'Only the persons involved,' I promised.

With the complainant's cheque and the defendant in tow, I headed for the courthouse. There, a confused clerk initially refused to accept the cheque until a senior clerk convinced him that the complainant could in fact pay a fine for the person who had offended against him. The senior clerk's final remark was, 'McCafferty must be a big man.'

McCafferty wasn't in great spirits when I returned to the shop. I could only thank the grocer and add that the boy's mother had promised to pay the fine back at ten shillings a week. 'They have trouble paying their grocery bills around here, never mind anything extra,' was his disgruntled reply.

Saor Éire was a breakaway group of IRA volunteers who had harkened to the Bogside's call for help when Ian Paisley and Ronald Bunting issued their threats. Most of them arrived after the fighting was over and, although the Defence Association knew about them, we played down their presence in the Bogside. We found accommodation for them in the corrugated-iron pavilion at Celtic Park. Here they set up a field kitchen. They were resourceful and independent. They more or less kept their own counsel. Every morning they performed the ceremony of raising the tricolour. Although their numbers never exceeded a dozen, their presence gave rise to Paisley's allegation that there was a trained army within the Bogside. With the exception of the tall, bearded Seán Doyle, who seemed to be their leader, I had very little contact with them. My go-between was Keenan, who appeared to know a number of them personally. Seán Doyle had arrived exhausted from his native Dublin, and Eileen gave him one of our children's beds. Laying himself down with a blanket over his huge frame, his beard at one end of the bed and his boots sticking out over the other, he was an awesome sight. Later, while travelling in the West Indies, I had the privilege of meeting an Irish lady who had settled there who told me that Seán Doyle had been her childhood sweetheart. I would come to appreciate this man and his followers, who had put the unity of the country above all else. They forwent personal comfort, money and status in pursuit of the ideal of an united Ireland.

Such idealism was common in the Bogside; the Defence Association met at least every other night in full session to deal with the affairs of the area. Our members assumed responsibility for various matters such as transport, billeting, social affairs and defence. The association was jealous of its autonomy and aware of its responsibility. There was a very high level of attendance at the meetings. The standard of debate would have done credit to any elected body of representatives. Keenan and I implemented the decisions of the association and were strictly monitored by the general body. Very few decisions were made without the full sanction of the governing body. However, in the course of our leadership we did take a few decisions without consulting the committee.

As soon as the fighting ceased, many politicians visited Derry. One of them was Conor Cruise O'Brien. I had followed his career with interest and pride. He had held a post with the United Nations and was now a member of the Irish Labour Party. As he had taken part in civil-rights demonstrations in America, I assumed that he would sympathise with our struggle in Northern Ireland. After Haughey's show of belligerence and Lynch's promise not to stand by, I hoped for something positive from one of the leading lights in the resurgent Irish Labour Party.

As we talked, I began to realise that national support for our struggle was less than total. We had the sympathy of the world, but the people we had traditionally looked to for practical support – the Irish government – were powerless to help.

In a clipped, cultured accent, which I had great difficulty in placing – he sounded almost like an educated Englishman – O'Brien described the lonely life of the international politician. He brushed aside the idea that the UN would intervene on behalf of the Irish government. He was held to be an expert on the UN, having represented it in various war zones around the world. Upset at his abrupt manner, I pressed him once again on the possibility of international intervention. O'Brien responded: 'Of course! The Irish government can appeal to the United Nations and they will get a certain amount of mileage out of it, but Britain is an expert in that sphere of operation, and there will be a counter-move. The Irish government can then come back, and the sparring will continue, each one playing the game according to the rules, and each one knowing the limitations of the system. But at the end of the day, it will never get as far as the Security Council.'

I was getting angry now: 'We're not interested in playing games. What we want to know is, if we are attacked here and people are killed, what will the Irish government do?'

'Nothing,' he replied instantly. Then, as if upon reflection, he added, 'Of course, I can't speak for the Irish government but I do believe they can and will do nothing'.

For me, this was the last straw: 'I don't know why you and your friends came the whole way from Dublin. You must be very busy men. We are also busy and it's about time you left, so that we can get on with our work.'

People were arriving from all over the world. To young French students, Free Derry was a resurrection of the Paris Commune. A Russian journalist who had lost a foot at the Battle of Stalingrad thought that we were fighting a people's war against capitalist oppression. The British press considered us to be an affront to civilisation. There was freedom of speech in Free Derry and all sorts of ideologies were trotted out at street corners. The drinking houses were open all hours. My remarks to the effect that 'The writ of the English Queen no longer runs in Free Derry' angered the British establishment and caused Paisley to foam at the mouth while addressing a gathering of his disciples in the Waterside. 'King of the Bogside!' he screamed. 'I'll tell you what he is: Scum of the Bogside!'

Social work took up a good deal of our time. I often had to visit Bundoran, a seaside town on the west coast, to care for the refugees housed in the army camp there. One young refugee had charmed one of the Irish soldiers there and their relationship was creating tensions among the soldiery. I was asked to come down to help sort things out. I walked through the camp with an officer who stood over six feet tall and dwarfed me. 'My God, we should have taken Derry. There are 800 of the finest fighting men in Ireland here and for a full forty-eight-hour stretch we worked like men possessed preparing for the invasion. Not one word of protest from any one of them. When Lynch made his "We can no longer stand by" speech, we thought, "This is it."

Oh, the frustration, the disappointment. Why the orders to go in were not given, we will never know. Every one of them would have given his life to free the North and now all they can fight over is a young girl, fleeing with her child in fear of being murdered,' he raged.

It turned out that the young girl was not as frightened as the officer thought. She had developed a relationship with a soldier and she defied the O/C to move her out of the camp. She challenged us both: 'Your job is to look after the refugees from the North, and if you put me out of the camp there will be hell to pay'.

After several hours of heated arguments with the young mother, the three of us came to a resolution: the O/C would not discipline the soldier if she agreed to leave. I promised to find her a safe place to live in Derry. That night I drove her back to Derry, away from her lover. If only Jack Lynch had had a little of her passionate determination, then our dream of liberation might have become a reality. During a few hours of discussion that night, I learnt that the troops had been instructed to hold their fire and consolidate their position if they were confronted by British troops when crossing the border with an invasion force.

Our idealism waned a little in the carefree atmosphere of Free Derry. The Defence Association had naively abandoned the idea of social control in the belief that, freed from the restraints of Stormont and its oppressive machinery, people would behave differently. They didn't. But in the main, people were friendlier than usual and more hospitable than their meagre resources could bear. Everyone was welcome and many undercover American and British secret agents had food and beds to come back to after a long day of sniffing around. But the petty thieves and conmen didn't change their ways. The people were in a more trusting mood and the pickings were easier. People caught carrying out petty crimes would be tried by Seán Keenan. He told them of his vision of a new Ireland and would spend hours patiently trying to persuade the budding criminals to mend their ways and have more concern for others.

I was overwhelmed with work and always on a short fuse. I exploded when the same people appeared before me for the umpteenth time to express contrition for their crimes. We had managed to establish a degree of law and order in Free Derry which demonstrated to the outside world that we could look after ourselves without supervision. But the order – the parallel state we had created and were trying to hold together – was a fragile thing. We had no police force, and no code of law to refer to. I felt that the initial flush of idealism in Free Derry had peaked and was waning. Without resources or guns, the association now found itself in the position of having to govern a community and deal with mundane matters such as hooliganism. What were we to do with criminals? Thieves – like the guy I saw pushing a copper boiler down the street – were helping themselves to whatever they wanted. We had no detention centres. I grew so desperate at one stage that I even asked the Irish army to let us have a house in Donegal to use as a prison. At the beginning we let publicans keep premises open for as long as they wanted. They did, and as result drunks were fighting and roaring in the streets at all hours of the night. The only solution was to enforce a closing time, although our pubs stayed open for an hour longer than drinking-houses in the rest of Northern Ireland.

I heard a report that a young girl had been raped somewhere in the Bogside. The rape of a child is the most terrible thing that can befall a family or a community. I ordered two separate groups of men to arrest the rapist and bring him to Number 10, but he turned himself in. He knocked on my door, a slight, thin, unshaven man in his early thirties with long, lank hair. 'I believe you're looking for me,' he said. He came inside and, standing before me, he recited the details of his crime. As he talked, I realised the enormity of what he had done, and how unprepared I was for dealing with a crime of this order. I convened a court and agreed to preside over it. He repeated his description of his crime and made no attempt to deny his guilt. His defence counsel entered a plea for leniency on his behalf. I looked at the faces of the jurors, wondering what we going to do with him. We, the DCDA, had eschewed any contact with the RUC and had placed ourselves outside the established legal system. He was our problem to solve and we had to satisfy the community's demand for his punishment. I suddenly felt a sense of loneliness in the position of authority which I had assumed. The jury unanimously ruled that he was guilty. 'What sentence do you pass?' I asked them.

'Death,' each one replied.

The finality appalled me: was execution the appropriate punishment? Suddenly I heard myself saying that the people who had suffered most at his hands – the girl and her family – should decide the rapist's fate. I summoned the child's mother to appear before the court. Ten minutes or so later, a teenage girl – she was maybe eighteen or nineteen – came to the door. She was the child's sister; her distraught mother had asked her to represent the family. The rapist sank to his knees before her, pleading for mercy, his hands joined in supplication.

The girl uttered only one sentence. 'I hate this man for what he has done to my sister, but I cannot agree that he should be put to death.' I turned to the rapist. 'In deference to the wishes of this young woman and her family, the court has spared your life.' I pointed to one of the men present. 'Should you molest a child again, this man will execute you without warning.'

A life had been saved, but a rapist had gone unpunished. Having turned in that night, I lay shaking in bed for several hours before sleep came to me.

Canavan appointed a one-eyed American to the post of chief of police. The American had come to the area about a year earlier, claiming to be a reporter for the *Potsdam Courier*. At the Scarman Tribunal he had presented valuable photos showing a combined force of policemen and militant Orangemen attacking the Bogside. He had been shot at while driving though a checkpoint manned by B-Specials when on his way to supply medical dressings for the people behind the barricades.

We never discovered whether the *Potsdam Courier* actually existed, and no one ever substantiated the rumour that the American had lost his eye during the Arab-Israeli war in 1967. But he was a good chief of police. The black patch over his sightless eye gave him the look of a buccaneer. His appearance and his exploits gave him an air of authority. The crime-detection rate increased as he and his lieutenants – one an Englishman, the other a Limerickman, both domiciled in Derry – went about their work. They carefully documented every incident and name. Nevertheless, I wasn't particularly happy about having them around. I didn't like their methods of detecting crimes, either: their philosophy was 'set a thief to catch a thief'. I was fiercely parochial in my outlook, so it upset me to see security in the hands of three strangers. 'Cyclops' based himself a few doors down from Number 10 and had a telephone installed. My insistence that his telephone merely be an extension of my own angered the American. He believed that I did not trust him. And he was right.

Another problem faced the Defence Association. We had defended the Bogside with sticks, stones and petrol bombs. If the army, which had us surrounded, moved against us, we would be finished. We had no weapons and even if we had had them, no one would have known how to operate them. Keenan and I went to the Irish army for help. The nearest Irish army post was Rockhill House, outside Letterkenny. The young sentry at the gate grew a little agitated on seeing the old red Morris Oxford with the Derry registration number. 'Is the commanding officer available?' I asked.

'No, but the officer in charge is up in the canteen,' he replied.

He didn't ask for our names and made no attempt to search the car. At the end of the driveway was Rockhill House, which was typical of the houses built by the landed gentry during the occupation. The canteen was full. I had an odd feeling as I shook hands with some of the officers. It had to do with the similarity between them and the British officers whom the Defence Association met regularly. I hoped I was mistaken. They all recognised Seán Keenan and me immediately and served us drinks – fruit juice for me and whiskey for Keenan.

The O/C was at the army headquarters in the Curragh, on the plains of Kildare, but was expected back soon. The afternoon wore on without any sign of him, and finally Keenan and I decided to leave for Derry. As we were saying goodbye to two officers at the door of the big house, a car drew up. I had no doubt that the man inside was the O/C. A powerful-looking man, Lieutenant Colonel Buckley exuded authority. He shook our hands and invited the two of us to his office.

Yes, he was well aware of the situation in Derry. His intelligence officers were in regular contact with people in the Bogside. Yes, they had considered the possibility of the British army attacking and taking Free Derry. The question was: what could he do for us? We had two requests: we wanted a large house somewhere in Donegal as a detention centre for young offenders and we needed training in small arms for the men of Derry. There was a long silence. The O/C of the Northern Command of the Irish army shook his head in disbelief. His sympathy went out to the people of the North, but in no way could the army get involved in the ways we had requested.

There was an embarrassed silence. I broke in: 'Will you send the request up the line?'

There was a look of relief on the O/C's face. 'Certainly, but it will take several days to get an answer.' From the look on his face, he believed that the answer would be negative.

We drove back to Derry in silence. Keenan had nothing but contempt for the Irish establishment and obviously felt he had compromised himself again by seeking its help. I, believing that the Irish government's concern was genuine, hoped for a positive response to our request. I knew that the O/C in Letterkenny would give a full report on the meeting to his superiors, and that our request would be dealt with at the highest level. Only a political decision could activate the army in the way that I wanted. Less than a week later, a telephone call summoned me to Rockhill Barracks. An officer whom I had never met before told me to 'prepare my men for military training'.

The Defence Association boxed very cleverly in its negotiations with the British army. Canavan was our principal negotiator. With his sharp, analytical mind, he was more than a match for any soldier. Often when negotiations were deadlocked, he produced a formula which satisfied the British on the one hand and allayed the fears of the Defence Association on the other. Michael was not involved in negotiations with the Irish army. As we did with the rest of the Defence Association, Keenan and I kept him in the dark about our work in this area. Now, though, we had to take some of the members into our confidence if we were to take full advantage of the chance to train with the Irish army. I talked to Canavan and studied him as he mulled over the consequences of having young men trained in the use of arms. We were living on a knife-edge and Canavan knew that, in the event of a total breakdown, sweet talking would not protect the people. I sighed with relief when he nodded his head in assent. Having secured his agreement, I urged him to sign up for weapons training. 'Give me a few days to think about it,' he replied.

I was unreserved in my admiration for Michael Canavan as a negotiator and also because he had played football with me, worked with me in the credit-union movement and stood shoulder to shoulder with me during the civil-rights agitation. If I had to choose a man with whom to enter a difficult and challenging situation, I wouldn't have to think for long. Canavan's agreement to join the armed defence of the people would be of extreme importance. Four days later, Canavan said to me, 'Put my name down for military training.'

The first batch of men to be trained by the Irish army were chosen with considerable care. I knew that the Irish government would be severely embarrassed if it became known that men from the North were being trained in the use of firearms. Everyone was briefed on the need for secrecy. My two sons, my elder brother and six others working out of Number 10 formed the first unit.

Although claiming constitutional jurisdiction over the territory of Northern Ireland, the government of the Republic did accept that Northern Ireland was, de facto, a separate state. This paradox was rooted in the Anglo-Irish Treaty of December 1921. One of the arguments for the acceptance of the Treaty was that it would lead to the creation of a twenty-six-county state with its own institutions and army. These, then, would have as their primary purpose the reunification of the country. This 'stepping-stone' theory necessitated accepting the unacceptable – the Treaty – as a means of eventually obtaining freedom. The vision of future unity sustained us during the dark years of conflict and discrimination.

General Michael Collins was the principal exponent of the stepping-stone-theory policy and was one of the signatories to the Treaty. I believed that had Collins not been assassinated, he would have actively pursued unity by force of arms. Many of the Northerners who joined the Free State army in 1922 were convinced that they would eventually move against Northern Ireland. But civil war broke out in the South and the bitter divisions which characterised the infant state distracted politicians and soldiers from the pursuit of national unity.

My mind then wandered to Éamon de Valera, now the President of Ireland. He had been one of the leaders of the defeated Republican side in the civil war. He had been in the political wilderness for a number of years afterwards. In 1926, de Valera left Sinn Féin and founded Fianna Fáil. In the general election of 1932, that party swept all before it. Once in power, Dev began to undermine the Treaty. He turned the Oath of Allegiance into a dead letter and regained control of Irish ports. He also withheld the land annuities (annual payments made by Irish farmers to the British government). Within a few years of de Valera's accession to power, many issues seemed to have been resolved to the satisfaction of the majority of the people of Ireland. Only partition remained. And now, if the elected government of Ireland was unable – or unwilling – to address the national question, then others, who put the reunification of Ireland before anything else, would.

My historical musings ended as the car came to a halt outside the temporary recruitment building in Buncrana, twelve miles from Derry. We were greeted by Captain Pat McGonagle, who supervised our registration for arms training. No one ever swore the oath of allegiance to the Irish Republic more sincerely than we did. By joining the *Fórsa Cosantais Áitiúil*, a part-time force similar to the British Territorial Army, we made ourselves eligible for weapons training. Any Irish citizen was entitled to join the FCA, and when trouble broke out in Northern Ireland, men all over the country flocked to the colours. We used our real names but invented bogus Donegal addresses. My brother and I had to knock ten years off our ages to satisfy the regulations. After half a century, the training of Northern

Irishmen for action in Northern Ireland had resumed. Within a few days we were ordered to report for training to Dunree Fort on the shores of Lough Swilly.

The nine of us stood there, shirts in our hands. Two men were bare-chested; the others were wearing various types of singlets. The compulsory medical inspection began. With an unlit cigar in his mouth, the doctor pushed his stethoscope against the men's white skin. 'Pass! Pass!' He came to my eldest brother. 'Too much smoking and drinking. Pass.' The formalities over, the doctor re-lit the shredded end of his cigar. 'I could do with a good drink,' he quipped, perhaps in sympathy with my elder brother. Or maybe the remark reflected his disbelief at what was happening. I reported for duty every morning but was allowed to return to Derry in the evening while the other men remained in the camp.

One Thursday, I arrived at Dunree and found the place deserted, except for the guard at the gate. It was so quiet that I could hear the slap of the waves against the rocks. I walked across the parade ground, my footsteps echoing in the early morning air. I surveyed the motley collection of huts huddled together in the fortress on the edge of Europe and thought, 'Hell! What a place to be in wintertime!' The British had built similar forts all over the world. I had to admire their soldiers' ability to deal with life in these places. I remembered, when I was very young, seeing pictures in the *Derry Journal* of British troops leaving this fort and Irish soldiers replacing them. Someone must have realised that there wasn't much point in having soldiers in this godforsaken place. Who would want it, anyway, with its rocks, heather, deep-seated problems and un-manageable people?

I went up to the Officers' Mess. The table was set for breakfast, but there was no one around, not even a cook. I was heading for the firing range when I met a soldier hurrying across the parade ground. 'Where is everyone?' I asked.

'At Mass. Today is the feast of Our Lady and she's the patron saint of the army,' the soldier explained. I followed him to the small chapel, where the entire garrison was kneeling at prayer. Mass had not yet started. I stood at the back. I felt out of place in my short-belted overcoat among the uniformed officers and men. The O/C was kneeling on a prie-dieu before the two steps leading to the altar. He turned around to look at the newcomers. I was trying to make myself as inconspicuous as possible but he caught sight of me. He got up, picked up a prie-dieu which had been leaning against the wall, placed it beside his own and beckoned me to kneel beside him. Our kneeling together in the simple chapel in Ireland's most northerly military base seemed to symbolise a unity of purpose between us. The occasion meant more to me than the promises of politicians and civil servants. I wasn't to know that before the week was out, devious politicians and civil servants would be doing their damnedest to deny that we had ever been there, and that the army would quote from the regulations to prove that we *could* never have been there.

Chapter 13

At least one of my visits across the border didn't involve military matters. I had a good relationship with a British Army officer who was based near me. He told me one day that he was due some local leave and wanted to see something of Donegal, so I arranged a day trip. Canavan also agreed to come along. The Inishowen 100 is a route around Inishowen over mountains, through boglands and past gleaming white beaches. Buncrana, Clonmany, Ballyliffin, Carndonagh, Malin and Moville are some of the towns along the way. The officer had difficulty getting his tongue around some of these place names but he was enthralled by the beauty of the countryside. After enjoying the magnificent views from the Gap of Mamore, we travelled down hairpin bends and stopped at a country pub.

The only customer in the bar was a man well into his seventies. He was only about five feet tall and the counter was level with the knotted scarf around his neck. The scarf, its ends tucked around the exposed braces holding up his trousers, looked as old as he was. His sparkling eyes indicated a mind that age and drink hadn't dulled. He began drumming on the counter with a tumbler half-full of Guinness when we walked in. The noise brought the publican out from the depths of the house. Wiping the counter, he asked, 'What'll ye have, gentlemen?'

Canavan and I ordered orange juice and the officer ordered a whiskey.

'Irish or Scotch?' enquired the barman.

The officer hesitated and then, as if in deference to his companions, replied, 'I'll have a small Irish, please.'

The bar was too small for private conversation, not that

Michael and I desired privacy. We were very much at home in Inishowen; only the officer felt a little out of place. His civilian clothes, tan, well-cut cashmere overcoat, military bearing and English accent – not to mention his hesitant choice of whiskey – all registered with the old man. Referring to the whiskey, the old man raised his eyes and prayerfully intoned: '*Uisce Bheatha*, the Water of Life.' He waited until the barman had poured the whiskey and then continued, addressing the officer. 'Sir,' he said, 'you are about to taste the elixir of the gods – a drink which has had the spirit breathed into it by the little people of Ireland.'

As the officer raised the glass to his lips, the old man continued: 'Easy now, sir, treat it with respect. I remember many years ago, in the mountain under the shadow of which this house rests, men who had scant respect for the whiskey buried a twenty-five-gallon drum of it beneath the heather. In the hardness of their hearts, they cared for nothing but the money it would earn when it matured, but when they returned to taste the fruits of their labour, they discovered the spirit had been stolen by the little people.' I had heard this story before: the old man and his friends had visited the mountain by night, removed the maturing whiskey and replaced it with the brown, brackish water from the bottom of an excavated turf bank.

The officer was in a very relaxed and expansive mood on the return journey. He expressed how he'd felt when his regiment learnt it would be sent to Northern Ireland. 'A soldier has to be ready for active service: that's what soldiering is about and there is always excitement and expectation when the order comes. But active service inside the United Kingdom – none of us ever thought it could happen. Our orders were to secure the peace, but there were other elements in the situation as well. We were instructed that in the event of meeting Irish troops, we were to hold our fire and maintain our lines.'

The officer's disclosure bore out what I had heard in Donegal. The Irish had been ordered not to fire if they met British troops. Any lingering doubts in my mind about collusion between the Irish and British governments were now completely dispelled by the corroborative independent statements I had been given.

While enjoying a goodnight cup of coffee, we learnt the real reason why the officer had wanted a day out with us. He began quizzing us about politics. Before he left, he had this to say on the situation in Northern Ireland: 'I believe people like you will never accept the British occupation of Northern Ireland, and the present relationship between the Catholics and the army will end in confrontation. Inside the next couple of years, the British army will be in this country in massive numbers and that will begin the decolonization of Northern Ireland. I have seen this happen in many countries throughout the British Empire and the pattern is always the same. I have seen it repeated here, and the process, having started, will never be reversed.'

The Bogside was invaded by British soldiers on a few occasions. We expected the odd covert intelligence-gathering incursion, but we had never bargained for incursions by individual soldiers. I was stretched out on top of the bed when a young man with close-cropped hair entered my room, escorted by two of our security men. He snapped to attention, saluted and gave his name, rank and serial number. 'I have come to join the forces of Free Derry. I'm an expert in small arms. Can you use me?' he asked, in a soft, Southern accent.

'What the hell do you do with a British soldier who has gone AWOL, especially when he turns up in your bedroom?' I wondered to myself. It occurred to me that the army might come into the area looking for him; if it did, that would be the end of the truce. He may have been sick of soldiering, and be using us to get out of the army. After questioning him, I called up two

Gcars. The first would be a scout car, while the second would speed the deserter across the border. From Donegal he could return to his native county. He was the first British soldier to enter the area, and there would also be a second and third. Their stories were very different from his.

We had put some services in place to replace those withdrawn when the serious trouble began. We had a team of drivers who took the sick and injured to hospital. Hugh Breslin had just brought a sick person to Altnagelvin Hospital and was on the way back when he was flagged down by a man weighed down by what appeared to be a very heavy burden. Breslin stopped the car, reached over and opened the door on the passenger side. As he did so, he felt cold steel under his jawbone. The man said, 'Free Derry, quickly.' Breslin was so shocked he almost had a heart attack. The man dumped his bundle on the back seat. Several machine-gun magazines, two sub-machine guns and a number of pistols tumbled with dull metallic thuds onto the black leather. Breslin drove the car directly to my house and we went throught the name, rank and serial number routine once again. The weapons were welcome. I ordered them to be hidden away. With a certain amount of trepidation, I began questioning the soldier. The authorities may have been trying to set us up for a charge of possession of arms. After about an hour's interrogation, I was satisfied that the defector was genuine and that he had been following a plan devised by someone from Free Derry. I severely reprimanded the person who had initiated the operation without our permission and, worse still, hadn't kept to the arrangements he had made with the soldier. The latter, a young Irishman, must have been terrified: after stealing the weapons and climbing over the walls of Ebrington Barracks – where most of the soldiers based in Derry were stationed – he discovered that there was no one waiting for him. He had landed on the pavement in a predominantly Protestant area and was incredibly lucky to have selected Breslin's car.

I was afraid that the army would launch a full-scale search for him and foil our attempts to get him across the border. But the young Irish soldier assured me that we still had time. He explained that he had been down for communications duty that night and had arranged for another soldier from his home town to take his place at the communications centre. Their voices were quite similar. We had a few hours, until the time when he was due to be replaced, to get him out of Derry. I was amazed at his audacity and admired the Irish soldiers in the British army for their willingness to help us. The British military authorities would eventually give the matter some thought and decide that the Rhineland would be a more suitable posting for their Irish regiments. After finding a safe house for him across the border, I returned and enquired about the cache of arms. No one would tell me where it was and I began to realise that I hadn't as much control over things as I had thought. Seán Keenan and I would have to have a little talk.

Very early the next morning, Major Mike Reynolds phoned me, complaining that a soldier had gone missing. I listened with feigned sympathy, but I couldn't contain my amusement when Reynolds said, 'I wouldn't be so concerned, except the bloody bastard stole my personal pistol.' After I had raised the matter with Keenan, said pistol was returned to its owner.

The case of the third soldier was the most bizarre and frightening. It required all the energy and duplicity which I could muster, and exposed all the primitive emotions of a community under stress. It was a muggy evening at the end of a long, hot day. I was walking home when I heard a commotion. Men were streaming out of the headquarters, heading in the direction of the Lone Moor Road, shouting 'Laird! Laird!' I was about to follow them when I saw a man break away and run in the opposite direction. Instinctively, I followed him. He only became aware of me when I followed him into a house. He tried to conceal a revolver, while loading the chamber with bullets. As I struggled with him for possession of the weapon, he shouted, 'I'll kill the bastard!'

'Settle down. What the hell is happening?' I shouted back.

'It's Laird,' he said. 'He's in the area, and probably armed.'

Laird was something of a Protestant folk hero, and was a man to be reckoned with. He had been accused of attacks on young Catholics. There were a few Bogside men who would have relished the chance to get their hands on him. We knew that he had joined the British army. His sudden appearance behind the barricades in the Bogside sent a tremor of fear throughout the neighbourhood.

Having disposed of the gun, both of us ran in the direction of the crowd outside the home of Hugh Gallagher, a builder. Forcing our way through the agitated throng, which was growing larger by the minute, we got into the house and found out what had happened. Eddie Harrigan, who was on duty checking vehicles at the Marlborough Terrace barricade, had recognised Laird in a car. Before he could apprehend him, Laird got out and ran into the Bogside. Harrigan and the others on duty ran after him. Maureen Boyce, from her first-floor window, watched the chase, Laird running about ten yards ahead of his pursuers. He jumped the garden wall of the house next door and left his outline in the woven trellis fence surrounding the builder's yard. Maureen ran to my house in fright, but some poteen fresh in from Donegal calmed her down. The bottle was soon depleted, as other frightened people converged on Number 10. Hearing the shouting outside and believing that the army or police were after someone, Mrs Gallagher opened the door for the fugitive. The terrified Laird dashed into the house and hid himself in the cupboard under the stairs. One of our most difficult nights had begun.

As the news spread through the Bogside, the sound of running feet reverberated in the air. Laird was being interrogated.

He gave his name as McGarrigal, saying he was a soldier home on leave from England. People who appeared to know something about him contradicted this. Someone explained that his real name was indeed McGarrigal, but that he had been brought up by a family called Laird and had answered to that name all his life. The noise outside the house grew and the tension rose. Suddenly, the window of the living room shattered and a large granite set, such as was used in road-building before the invention of tarmacadam, landed on the floor. Even the toughest of us were afraid now. The crowd, now over a hundred strong, wanted Laird handed over. The people of the Bogside, who had behaved superbly and resolved to show that their struggle was above reproach, seemed to crack; a flood of emotion, which had been repressed as they awaited the outcome of political negotiations, burst forth.

I went outside. Shakespeare had summed it up a long time ago: 'A mob has no reason'. The crowd of respectable Bogsiders had indeed lost its reason. I saw the tall, bearded figure of Seán Doyle and said, 'Spread your men around the house. The man we are holding is a British soldier. If anything happens to him, we could feel the full weight of the British army very quickly.' The sight of the Saor Éire men spacing themselves around the house, facing the crowd, with hands on concealed weapons, had a sobering effect on the mob. I thanked God for the discipline of these men. Doyle and two others guarded the front entrance. The crowd was hurling abuse at Laird's protectors. It was like a scene from the film *In the Heat of the Night*. And the Saor Éire men could never have imagined that they would be facing down the Bogsiders in defence of a British soldier.

I phoned St Eugene's. Father Mulvey and another priest answered my call for help. They appealed to the people to disperse but the hatred of Laird was so intense that their pleadings were in vain. 'Go back to your church, Father! We want to hang the bastard!' the mob roared. Someone produced a rope and threw it over the crosspiece of a lamp standard. Father Mulvey, now standing on top of the brick gate-pier, was still pleading with them. I had given strict orders that no one was to enter the house to make contact with the captive. Only one man managed to breach the cordon. Leo Deehan, a former professional boxer who had been accused of membership of the IRA and possession of arms back in the 1940s, was the most fearless of the civil-rights marshals. As he forced his way into the house, I remembered that Deehan's son was one of those supposed to have been injured by Laird. Deehan was dying to work him over. He and I had been friends for years. I admired the honesty and courage he so often displayed in difficult circumstances. I took a chance: 'Leo,' I said, 'this prisoner must not be harmed and I am placing his safety in your hands.' I looked at Deehan, whose face was flushed with tension. He protested; I silenced him. 'Those are my orders. I expect them to be obeyed.' Deehan carried them out, showing great self-restraint.

We decided to contact Colonel Millman and have Laird checked out. After giving him a description, name, rank and number, we awaited his return call. 'Yes. Your investigations are correct. Trooper Thomas McGarrigal is on leave from Catterick Camp in England,' the colonel reported, going on to apologise on behalf of the army for any inconvenience caused. He requested the soldier's return. There was still shouting outside the house but the security team had held firm, and some of the older people had left. I knew it would be a few more hours before we were out of the woods. 'We will turn him over to you at the William Street barricade at dawn,' I told Millman.

Keenan had been questioning the soldier while I negotiated. He found that he was carrying receipts for petrol bought at a filling station near RTÉ in Dublin on the same day that a bomb had exploded at the television complex. We took tea a few times during the night. Although the prisoner drank what he was offered, he never relaxed during his captivity. As dawn approached, only a few diehards remained outside the house, and I began preparing for the handover. We used three cars. Deehan, two others and I went in the middle car with our captive and headed for the barricade in William Street. The pale light of dawn disclosed a strong military force at William Street. We stopped the car about fifty yards from dozens of soldiers, several heavy military vehicles and jeeps with machine guns mounted. Colonel Millman was in charge. We escorted Laird to the barricade. A Sergeant Soby issued a receipt, and Trooper Thomas McGarrigal, alias Thomas Laird, was duly handed over to the British army. The Defence Association had prepared its own document. 'Received one male live body, Trooper Thomas McGarrigal' was the wording. Soby completed the document with his signature.

After this short, unexpected lapse into near-barbarism, the community returned to normal the following day. The newspapermen who had slept during the night hours could not add substance to the rumours that something extraordinary had happened. They failed to prise any information from those involved. Just as people suppress memories of a drunken indiscretion, the people of the Bogside put the whole business to the backs of their minds. Gallagher, the builder, when asked about his broken window, would reply, 'What broken window?'

Life had its funny side, too. The Defence Association met one evening in a room which was full to capacity. Forty delegates had come from previously unrepresented areas of Free Derry. The increased membership and all the different points of view within the Association made decision-making very difficult. I was chairing the meeting. I missed Keenan, the usual chairman. His extramural activities were taking up more and more of his time, leaving me to look after the day-to-day running of the organisation. The matter under discussion was a car which had been damaged at a temporary, unlit barricade: who was to pay for the repairs?

A member of the Peace Corps interrupted the meeting. 'There's a young boy outside who wants to see you,' he said.

'Get someone else to see him,' I replied.

Within minutes he was back: 'He won't talk to anyone but you.'

I turned to Paddy Johnston. 'Go out and deal with that matter and stop these interruptions.'

Johnston returned. 'It's no use. He won't talk to anyone but you and refuses to go away.'

Burdened with work and full of a sense of my own importance, I rose with exasperation and went to the front door, where a ten-year-old boy was waiting for me. He taught me what Free Derry was all about. 'What do you want?' I asked.

'I've lost my budgerigar,' said the boy.

I wasn't sure I had heard him right. 'What's that you said?'

'I've lost my budgerigar,' he repeated.

Anger at the youngster's audacity began to well up inside me. I was about to send him packing when the significance of the situation dawned on me. For years I had been telling people to get off their knees and demand justice. The boy had lost his pet bird and was appealing to the highest authority he knew for help. 'How did it happen?' I asked.

'My mother accidentally left the door of its cage open when she was feeding it and it flew out through the open window and eventually got into one of the high flats.'

'Did you enquire from the tenants of the flats if they had the bird?' I asked.

'I did, and they have it, but won't return it,' replied my young tutor in the art of dealing with authority.

My sense of priorities now corrected, I signed an order: 'Please release one budgerigar immediately,' and sent two members of the Peace Corps with the boy to collect his pet. On the veranda of the fourth floor of the Rossville Street flats, the two watched as the young boy formally handed over the order to the woman of the house where the bird had taken up residence. She immediately complied. Justice was done and seen to be done.

CHAPTER 14

Free Belfast didn't have the carefree atmosphere of Free Derry, nor was it a cohesive area. It took in twenty-three barricaded-off Catholic areas of the city. The defence association representing these areas had an enormous and complex task. Free Derry had prepared for an attack; Free Belfast had not. With Jackie Lavelle, a Belfast community worker I walked through areas devastated by loyalist violence. In the morning sunlight, the windowless openings in the burnt-out houses looked like empty eye sockets, and the rows of pointed apexes like sharpened teeth.

Jackie Lavelle related the terrible details of the latest pogrom against the Catholics of Belfast. It must have been impossible to stop the Orange mobs overrunning the scattered ghettos, because the RUC, armed with heavy machine guns, had joined the mobs and poured hundreds of rounds of ammunition into the tiny houses and the high-rise flats, killing a number of people. The Battle of the Bogside was a picnic compared with the terror unleashed on the Catholics of Belfast.

I stopped at a gable on which someone had added a few letters to the slogan 'IRA' so that it read 'I Ran Away'. I thought of Peter Pan moving his phantom battalions around. We came across an elderly woman and a young girl poking through the charred remains of furniture in one of the burnt-out houses. The woman coughed and her body shook as the acrid air attacked her nostrils and throat. She bent over, resting her hands on the remains of a kitchen sofa, but couldn't stop coughing. The sounds disturbed the eerie quietness of the street, which days before had hummed with energy. The young girl stepped quickly through the burnt-out debris, put her arms around the older woman's wasted body, placed her cheek on the woman's shoulder and gently rocked her. Then the two victims of sectarian hatred parted to continue their search. 'She lived there for twenty years and has lost everything,' Lavelle said in an undertone, before introducing me as 'the man from Derry'. Her eyes were clouded with tears which refused to flow, denying her a little relief. She added substance to the graffiti, saying, 'They weren't there when we needed them. Thank God some of the old hands were around. Without them we would all have been killed.' As Lavelle later explained: 'When it became obvious that the IRA was non-existent, a few of the men who had campaigned during the 1940s and 1950s gathered what weapons were available. They dashed from street to street firing short bursts, first at one end and then at the other, to create the illusion that the area was well defended. The guns became red-hot as they blasted their message of defiance into the darkness. There were no identifiable targets and no hits were claimed but the noise was sweet music to the ears of those who had thought that their abandonment would end in death.'

'Grandma,' the young girl said, holding a bundle of charred envelopes with their insides gutted and brown. 'There are no photos left, but maybe some of the letters are all right.' The old lady carefully took the brittle offering into her soot-blackened hands and her tears began to flow. Lavelle and I moved away, pretending to be concerned about a dangerously overhanging piece of masonry. 'Her man died fifteen years ago,' said Lavelle. 'He had spent many years on the building sites of Birmingham and London. The little one is her granddaughter.' We turned to take our leave from the distraught couple. The woman had composed herself, and with quiet determination she looked into my eyes and said, 'Twice before in my lifetime I was driven out, but I will never run again.'

I had another appointment to keep in a part of Belfast far from the burnt-out buildings. I approached a gracious, well-maintained old house which was owned by some friends of mine. I removed my coat in the oak-panelled hallway and looked at the antique furnishings in the room beyond. There was no alcohol available, but glasses of fruit juice helped to ease the awkwardness of formal introductions.

Among the guests was the Minister of Home Affairs, Robert Porter. I remembered him from a previous meeting during which he had defended the Special Powers Act. As my hand, hardened by years in construction work, shook his, I noticed how soft his hand was. This son of working-class Protestant parents from the Hill of Creggan was now one of the most important and powerful ministers in the government. The courses our lives had taken said a lot about society. I had been a good student at school but had had to leave before my fourteenth birthday to take up whatever employment I could find. The minister had gone to grammar school and university and had served in the army and in the Northern Ireland judiciary before entering politics.

The dinner was a genteel affair – a far cry from the soup of the Bogside. Everyone avoided mentioning the political situation. As we retired to the other room for coffee, I broke away and phoned Derry. Keenan told me that Derry was quiet. I hadn't informed him, or anyone else, that the friends I was visiting in Belfast had arranged my meeting with the minister. I had been approached by my old friends, who had dedicated their lives to the cause of peace. In the main they were Protestants, but they abhorred the treatment of Catholics and sincerely believed, even at this late hour, that peace could be restored. But any arrangement was doomed to failure. I would experience unionist intransigence and gain an insight into the unionist leaders' unshakeable belief in their right to rule.

After we had had our coffee, the other guests left the minister and me alone. We settled down to talking politics. After some verbal sparring, testing each other's positions, the minister said, 'Mr Doherty, in a democratic state the majority rules.'

I countered, 'I thought that democracy meant that everyone would get a fair crack of the whip.'

'We will treat everyone fairly, but in the final analysis, the majority makes the decisions,' replied the man who, a short time before, had allowed the use of CS gas against the people of his own city.

I switched my attack, saying, 'Fifty per cent of all the children going to primary school now are Catholics. In the normal course of events, they will eventually form the majority of the population of Northern Ireland. It may take twenty years, or even fifty, but the inevitable change will come.'

The face of this usually unflappable man betrayed agitation and indignation. Then, speaking for the Protestant people, he said, 'I love the queen. I fought for her, and we will never allow this state to be part of a united Ireland.'

My final thrust brought the fruitless debate to a close. 'You appear to use the democratic ethic when it suits you and would ignore it in the future as you have ignored it in the past. It looks as if we will have to fight even when we become a majority. If that is the case, we should fight now and end it.'

On 12 September Lord Cameron, a Scottish judge, delivered a 100,000 word report on his investigation into the disturbances during the early part of the year. The report savaged the Unionist government and the Orange Order and praised John Hume for his work in the interests of peace. That other aristocrat, Sir Leslie Scarman, had already set up his tribunal of enquiry into the cause of the August riots, and Lord Hunt, who had scaled Mount Everest, was given the more formidable task of investigating and reshaping the RUC. Sir Harold Hinsworth was appointed to investigate the effects of CS gas. Northern Ireland was collapsing while noble lords probed the causes of the Troubles.

On Monday 22 September, Justice Scarman began to take evidence in Derry. I was appointed by the Defence Association to sit in on the tribunal and assist our lawyers. During the first week, I was introduced in the foyer of the courthouse to Desmond Boal QC. Boal was a Derryman, retained by the Apprentice Boys to look after their interests during the course of the hearings. 'Go easy on the Apprentice Boys,' he said jokingly to me.

I replied, 'I will crucify them if I can.'

Quick as a flash, Boal shot back: 'Build a cross for yourself while you're at it.'

I had taken a strong liking to the small, dark man and felt an affinity with him. It was a pity we were on opposite sides. The Defence Association was represented by Liam McCollum QC, another Derryman. McCollum was probably one of the descendants of settlers who came over from Scotland to conquer the natives on behalf of Elizabeth I.

My relationship with Hume had been close over the years. I could read his mind like a book. As we sat in the corner of the front room in Number 10, talking about nothing in particular, I waited patiently for Hume to get to the point of his visit. 'When do you think you will be giving evidence before the tribunal?' Hume asked.

'Soon, I hope,' I replied.

'They are very thorough; you will need to be careful,' he remarked, almost casually.

'I have nothing to hide,' I retorted with annoyance.

'What about your visit to the Irish government and the promise of help?' he queried.

'I will not be volunteering any information, but if I am asked a direct question under oath, I will not tell a lie,' I pledged.

'If the information becomes public knowledge, it could cause serious embarrassment to the Irish government and may even result in violence.'

I gritted my teeth in anger and swore, 'For God's sake, John! Get off my back!'

I believe I was the last person to be called by the Scarman tribunal in Derry. I spent the afternoon of one day and the forenoon of the next in the witness box. I answered the questions truthfully, at length when it suited me, and was abrasive and confrontational on inconsequential issues, wasting the time available to the tribunal. When the QC for the Crown accused me of being the hard man of the DCDA, I rejected the accusation. There was an angry exchange, interrupted by Lord Scarman who leaned in my direction. 'Would you accept that you were one of the hard men?' I conceded that that was true. I liked Scarman, and agreed with a local woman who had sat in court every day during the hearings. 'There's more in that aul' head than a fine comb could take out.'

Captain Jim Kelly of the Irish Army phoned me the next day. The minister wanted to know if the training in Donegal of the men from Derry had been exposed. I was able to assure him that the matter had not been raised.

Bernadette Devlin was not the only one of us to visit America that year. Seán Keenan had also gone to fan the flames of Irish-American anger at the treatment of northern Catholics, but his visit was secretive, unlike hers. He wanted to conceal his absence from Derry from the authorities for a number of reasons, not least his need to secure his unemployment benefit, which he normally collected on Thursday. If it became known that he had made himself unavailable for work, the money would have been withheld. It was little enough, but he could not afford to lose it. I waited outside the labour exchange while he signed the necessary documents, then rushed him to Dublin Airport to catch the Aer Lingus flight to New York. I collected him the following week and got him back in time to sign on again.

He never told me whom he had met or what he had achieved during his visit, and I never asked. The gulf between us was widening. There was no bitterness between us: we simply realised that our different backgrounds and the different roads we had been travelling – which had temporarily converged during the defence of the Bogside – were again taking us in separate directions.

His motion 'that there should be no Hogg in our Bog' was defeated by sixteen votes to six, but McCann nonetheless threatened to organise opposition to the visit of Quentin Hogg, the Conservative Shadow Home Secretary. The army was concerned about the visit and was anxious to avoid a repetition of the Callaghan affair. Could the visit take place discreetly? After a tour of the city, Quentin Hogg repaired to RUC headquarters on the Strand Road. The gates slammed shut and the hacks were left to cool their heels outside. He was taken immediately to the rear entrance, where he got into a jeep. Major Reynolds accompanied him to the edge of the Bogside. Hogg then transferred to my car and within minutes was in Number 10. Keenan and Canavan were there. I introduced them and we got down to business.

Hogg claimed to have come to hear about the problems of the area but he insisted on speaking almost continuously for over an hour. His eyes twinkled mischievously as he opened his disquisition by stating that he intended to report to the Conservative Party conference the following week. Although he told us he would discuss any subject we wanted, he said he would stand over certain statements he made, while emphatically denying ever having made others if questioned by journalists. It was a light-hearted discussion. Hogg insisted that Catholics in Northern Ireland were exaggerating their woes and that their lives were considerably better than those of many other people throughout the world. Eileen served tea and chicken sandwiches. As Hogg made ready to leave, the hoodwinked newsmen arrived at the door.

Many other English politicians would pay us a visit, but Callaghan and Hogg seemed closest to the Establishment, which was only prepared to nibble at the edges of the problems besetting the Northern state. It would not accept fundamental changes unless forced to. Keenan was too courteous to say, 'I told you so'. He lost interest in meeting British officers or politicians and husbanded his energies for the inevitable confrontation with the British forces.

The reasoning behind the policy of avoiding this confrontation was very simple. They had an almost inexhaustible supply of modern weapons with the manpower to use them; we had neither. The political reason was to hold the moral high ground while Jim Callaghan, the British Home Secretary, negotiated his proposed changes for the future of the Six Counties with the Unionist government. We were acutely aware that this was going to be difficult and might prove to be impossible. However, we had to hold our nerve and allow the process to take its course.

The British brigadier who was in charge of the area was an important element in this strategy. I believed that he was genuinely concerned about the inequalities existing under the Unionist regime and he seriously believed that the removal of those inequalities would solve the political problems. He was appalled at the level of unemployment among young men and attracted public attention to the desperate need to create jobs. Not once during his tour of duty did he refuse to meet with the Defence Association representatives when asked to do so. He was always courteous and helpful, and he never reneged on any commitment he made to the Defence Association. I liked the man.

Our brigadier acquaintance got in touch to tell us that he would shortly be returning to England, and that he wanted to meet us again before he left. We arranged an evening in Michael Canavan's house. Derry was safe enough at that time for a British officer: the IRA, in the midst of its latest split, was a threat only to itself. He spoke with fondness about Ireland, saying how beautiful the countryside was and how much he had enjoyed himself here. Then he switched to another of his favourite subjects: food. He wondered why Irish food was so poor. How could the Irish make such a mess of cooking when they had the finest natural ingredients at their disposal? Eileen Canavan listened with growing irritation. 'This country could learn something from the Italians or the French,' the brigadier continued. Eileen left the room, reappearing about ten minutes later. 'Listen, Brigadier,' she announced, 'I'm not about to let you go back to England to put it about that you never had a good meal in Ireland.' She had booked a table for midnight at the Roneragh House, a smart restaurant over the border in Fahan. We drove off in Michael's car. That he was breaking military rules by crossing the border didn't seem to concern the brigadier, who was in charge of the British Army's Western Command in Northern Ireland.

We had a fabulous meal. Michael knew the owner of Roneragh House. He in turn must have had a word with his chef, who cooked as if the nation's honour depended on him. Course followed course. During the meal, I kept an eye on the brigadier, who was obviously in his element. Coffee was served. He leaned over to me and said in an undertone, 'You know, Mr Doherty, I've only earned one black mark during my time on duty in Derry.' I must have looked puzzled. 'Oh come on, Mr Doherty, those guns that were stolen from Ebrington Barracks . . . we traced them to your house.' He told me that he would not pursue the matter any further, provided I left the guns somewhere for collection the next day. I realised then that his chumminess was a cover, behind which he was trying to wrap up unfinished business. I looked the British officer squarely in the eyes. 'You must be mistaken,' I said, adding with perfect truth, 'I never touched those weapons.' I realised that the officer had had his own agenda when he accepted the invitation to dinner. He may have removed his uniform and left Northern Ireland, but he was still 'about his father's business'. This sharp altercation, unnoticed by the rest of the dinner party, was interrupted by the passing around of menus which we all autographed.

As the officer handed back the memento of his visit to the tiny village of Fahan in the shadow of the ancient Fort of the Hill of Grianan of Aileach, I noticed his cold, hard eyes. As I met his gaze, the mask of conviviality slipped and I caught a glimpse of the other side to the sophisticated and concerned Englishman. A cold shudder passed through my body and a premonition of what was to come seized me. I asked myself when the killing would begin.

The conversation turned to culture and literature. Eileen Canavan pointed in the direction of Grianan, to the ring fort overlooking Derry which had been the seat of power of Irish kings, lying at the centre of a sophisticated civilisation at the time that the brigadier's ancestors were struggling to throw off the Roman yoke. I had to pinch myself: here was a senior British commander sitting at a table with us in Donegal in the middle of the night being subjected to a lecture about the glories of Irish civilisation. I suppose that the four of us were trying to prove that we were unassailably in the right, that the Irish case was unanswerable. Anyway, in those early days we had nothing but words with which to oppose the British.

On 11 October the Russians put two men into space, and Pope Paul VI put the members of the Episcopal College in their place. He opened the extraordinary Synod of Bishops in Rome with the words *Pax Vobiscum* ('Peace be with you') and told them that his power was not conditional on their authority. The Defence Association was coming close to surrendering its authority to the

British. Callaghan arrived in Derry with Sir Arthur Young, whom he had appointed as the new Inspector General of the RUC. Peace was on the way. Callaghan didn't risk a repetition of his first visit: politicians, clergymen and representatives of tenants' associations went to a house in High Street, just inside the Bogside, to pay their respects to him. Despite Keenan's cynicism, I was beginning to feel stirrings of hope. The period since Callaghan's first visit had been one of great change. Callaghan had ordered the setting-up of a commission of enquiry under Lord Scarman to investigate the causes of the rioting. Two hundred and fifty thousand pounds was made available for victims of the Troubles, and nationalists arrested under the Special Powers Act were released without charge. The B-Specials were ordered to hand in their guns and the RUC was to be disarmed. Callaghan put civil servants into Stormont to supervise the changes. A community-relations minister would soon be appointed. Housing came under the control of central government and, from now on, need, rather than political considerations, would dictate housing policy.

The people on the streets were elated and were saying, 'Now is the time for the rebels to be generous to Britain's response to their demands for civil rights.' Even Eddie McAteer appealed for the Defence Association to hand over the keys of the Bogside to Callaghan in a final act of trust. I argued that the Defence Association would lose public support if it continued to defy all authority, and Keenan reluctantly agreed. He maintained that the nationalist people of Northern Ireland were a long way from understanding British duplicity, but that they would in the fullness of time. And he was right. But for now we could not resist the popular mood. The generals were also impatient for some movement. Brigadier General Leng had returned to England and it was now General Freeland who negotiated with the Defence Association. This small man, who had a twitch at the corner of his mouth, which created an illusion of a perpetual grin, had been dubbed 'Smiling Death' by his soldiers.

The barricades had come down in Belfast at the urging of Father Pádraig Murphy and Doctor Philbin, Bishop of Down and Connor. The Citizens' Defence Association there was conned into assisting the RUC and the army to retake the Catholic areas. The television news showed a white-armbanded Defence Association steward, flanked by a policeman and a soldier, walking the streets of Belfast's Catholic ghettoes, streets which had been 'no-go' areas only weeks earlier. Television also showed the worthy bishop being chauffeured around in an army jeep. These news images were astounding when one considered the suffering of the people of Belfast. Someone must have threatened them with eternal damnation or promised them everlasting life to persuade them to accept the police and the army back into their areas again. Perhaps it was just another act of trust. The sight of the three-man police force on TV shocked Keenan, Canavan and me. We knew that in their present generous mood, the people of the Bogside would not resist a forced entry by the army, even if the Defence Association condemned it. They felt that they had gone as far as they could during the preceding nine weeks; now it was time to negotiate.

We arranged a meeting with 'Smiling Death' in a Catholic school in the heart of the Bogside. He arrived in a military convoy and entered the room flanked by his aides. Canavan and I represented the Defence Association. Some members of the Tenants' Association, who had lately been arguing that they represented more people than the Defence Association, were also present. Keenan, who was now developing his own strategy, had given up on talks with the army. As I stood around waiting for the general, I decided to engage a well-tanned captain of the Military Police in conversation. The captain was gazing intently out of the window as I approached. He spoke first. 'What is that?' His finger was pointing at a tricolour floating gently in the breeze above the GAA pitch.

I replied, 'That's the Irish flag.'

'It has no right to be there,' said the captain.

'What price Callaghan's promise of a new society?' I thought to myself.

I shook hands with the general. His moniker was pretty close to the mark: his sallow skin stretched tightly over his small skull and his tic was pronounced. He wasted no time in getting the meeting started. Under the crucifix and the expressions of children's fantasies along the walls, men in khaki uniforms and sober suits talked. Freeland hoped that the Defence Association would help the RUC retake Free Derry. Canavan rejected this, pointing to the inability of the British government to bring about any real change in the attitudes of those who controlled Northern Ireland. The argument settled on the RUC's lack of impartiality and our demand that the force's uniform be changed. Freeland insisted that no police force could be asked to climb down to such an extent and still retain its authority and credibility. The tension in the room was rising. Canavan said, 'If they won't change the colour of their uniform there is little chance of a change of heart from the same people.'

The general sought to bring the debate to a close with the words, 'We have been very patient. We have remained out in the sticks for the past nine weeks and tomorrow we are going in.'

I watched Canavan's face turn white. In the measured tones he was wont to use when the chips were down, he said: 'General, we have been out in the sticks for the last fifty years and our patience has been exhausted. You can please yourself tomorrow and we will not attempt to influence the situation one way or the other, but . . . ' he paused and, adding emphasis by pushing his face closer to the mask on the other side of the table, continued, 'we will hold ourselves in readiness to answer to the wishes of the people. If they choose to reject you, we will back the people against you.'

I saw the amazement on the faces of the representatives of the Tenants' Association. Instead of the talks they had expected, they were watching an eyeball-to-eyeball confrontation. The skin on the general's skull stretched tighter and Canavan's face grew whiter. The representatives broke the tension by getting up from the table.

That evening the soldiers tried to break the deadlock and ingratiate themselves with the people by inviting the Tenants' Association to another meeting, to which no members of the Defence Association were invited. To their credit, the Tenants' Association delegates recognised that they were out of their depth, and declined the invitation. The policing function of the Defence Association was at an end. But under no circumstances would the Defence Association assist the police.

I was at home the next morning when three senior members of the Defence Association's police corps burst into my house. The tall, one-eyed American reached for the telephone beside me. I immediately seized his wrist: 'Who are you phoning?'

The American replied, 'The military police. We intend to phase in the policing operation mounted by the RUC and army.'

'The Defence Association gave specific instructions that no one was to assist the RUC or the army,' I replied.

'The Defence Association is finished! We are in charge,' said the man from the *Potsdam Courier*.

I rose from the chair and opened the door to the kitchen, where about ten young men were seated. 'Arrest both these men,' I said, pointing to the Englishman and the red-haired Irishman. 'Leave the Yank with me.' I returned to the room, where I began to question the American. I soon discovered that he had arranged to hand over to the police the complete set of records of the Defence Association police corps. These would have identified every person involved in criminal activities and exposed the running of the operation to the RUC. Angered by this treachery, I went to the kitchen and said, 'I have a difficult situation, and I need our friend to deal with it.' The implication was understood and one of the young men left immediately. Within minutes, 'our friend' entered the room and sat down. I related the circumstances and said, 'You will watch every move of this American during this day and if he makes an attempt to contact the police or army, shoot him dead!'

The colour of the one-eyed man's face turned a deathly white. He struggled to regain his composure. He made no attempt to justify his actions and agreed to remain under house arrest for two days. I went back into the kitchen and told the two prisoners: 'Your American friend has had a death sentence passed on him and if you don't want the same treatment, get the hell out of here and don't show your noses on the streets for the next twenty-four hours.' A detail was dispatched to strip the headquarters and the living quarters of the police corps of any item of information which might be of use to the RUC. The conspiracy to usurp the authority of the local leadership revealed a complete lack of understanding of the Bogside.

CHAPTER 15

Over Christmas, Derry remained relatively quiet. Although the Defence Association was officially defunct, Keenan and I kept an eye on developments. Neil Blaney, the Donegal man who was Minister of Agriculture in the Republic, sent us a message: 'Get up here as fast as you can.'

Keenan and I left early the next morning, wondering about the urgency of the message. The February frost slowed us down and we had plenty of time to discuss politics. Keenan was now an important member of the breakaway Provisional Sinn Féin movement. I was an unemployed builder who was negotiating for work with a British construction company in the West Indies. The honeymoon period with the army had lasted longer than both of us had expected but we agreed that violence was inevitable. The real issue in Irish politics, which we believed was the occupation of part of the country by Britain, would have to be addressed. On our first trip to Dublin we had worked out a strategy to impress our listeners. This was no longer necessary, since Blaney had proven beyond question his concern and his commitment to helping the nationalists of the North. Our relationship with him was quite close and was on an honest and open footing.

We were ushered into the minister's office upon our arrival. We shook hands and bantered while an aide prepared coffee. As we sipped coffee, the minister explained his concerns. The Irish army was re-equipping, in line with the other Western European armies, and some of the armaments it had disposed of had almost fallen into the hands of loyalist extremists. The disposal of arms was a pretty unregulated business. The only condition incumbent upon governments was that they export surplus arms; they could not be sold at home. Irish weapons were sold to an independent dealer outside the country. I was surprised to discover that Ireland had a role (however small) in increasing the number of armaments available throughout the world for killing people. Blaney told us that a Liverpool arms dealer had almost signed a contract to buy a massive number of .303 rifles with ammunition from the Irish government. Blaney had insisted that he be checked out before the deal went through. Intelligence reports indicated that the dealer was acting on behalf of Protestant extremists in Belfast and that, as soon as the armaments were bought, they would be sent to Northern Ireland. We were appalled.

Blaney wasn't cheered by what Keenan and I had to report. Implementation of the political reforms promised by the British government was proving well-nigh impossible. The Northern Ireland parliament was dragging its feet in the face of British pressure as Northern Ireland slipped closer to civil war. The Unionist establishment's denial of any need for reform was encouraging Catholics to believe that Britain would be unwilling, or even unable, to contain the trouble in future. We would have to defend ourselves.

We broke for lunch. I had never dined in the Shelbourne Hotel, nor anywhere as stylish and expensive as it was, and I enjoyed the experience. My shrimp cocktail came in a large silver goblet and was a superb opener for the steak dinner with all the trimmings. Keenan had wine, but not Blaney. I was surprised to hear the minister say that he had never taken alcohol in his life. He added with a twinkle in his eye, 'No one can ever accuse me of making a statement while under the influence of drink.' After the meal, he and I went to the men's room. While we were washing our hands, he adverted again to his discovery that Irish weapons had almost fallen into the hands of loyalists. 'These weapons should be made available to the Defence Association for the defence of our people in the North,' he said. 'The government has the right to sell them and the machinery for selling them. We can also supply the money,' he added.

Blaney had arranged for Charles Haughey, the Minister for Finance, to join us in his office after lunch. Haughey arrived within minutes of the resumption of the meeting. He was smaller than I had imagined, but I liked the cut of the man. He was fair-skinned, with strong, handsome features, and brimmed with a confidence bordering on arrogance. He was using a white handkerchief to dab at his nose. 'I have some sinus trouble,' he explained. After listening to the report from Keenan and me, he turned to Blaney and said, 'You better get Jim Gibbons down here immediately.' The names of two other members of the Cabinet came up. Kevin Boland was not available and Ó Morain, 'the man from Mayo', as they called him, was ill. Blaney and Haughey agreed that both would be sympathetic. Within minutes of Blaney's phone call, the Minister of Defence arrived.

Jim Gibbons was very tall and dark, with a swarthy complexion and a long hooked nose. He was relaxed on entering the room and, as he shook hands with Keenan and me, he showed no sign of surprise. Many delegations had come down from the North since we had dashed to Dublin on the eve of the Battle of the Bogside months earlier, and the advisability of involvement in the Northern troubles was a recurring theme in Southern politics. For the third time that day, specific issues relating to the North dominated our talk. We were most exercised by the attempt by Protestant extremists to accumulate arms. We also discussed the gun clubs set up by the disbanded B-Specials and the support they were receiving from Unionist MPs. We knew that the loyalists had about 100,000 legally held guns. The refusal of the Northern MPs to recognise the biased nature of the state, or to implement any real change, and the inability of

Britain to influence the situation, caused us grave concern. Another pogrom against the Catholic population in Northern Ireland was on the cards.

Charles Haughey, who had not spoken often during the meeting, addressed his two colleagues. 'Let's take the North. We should not apologise for what is our right.'

Gibbons shed his easy manner. Quickly he said, 'We couldn't. The army is 3,500 under establishment figures.'

That remark took us by surprise. But now the onus was on Gibbons to come up with a practical suggestion. 'I have ordered immediate recruitment to get the army up to strength and I am preparing for a doomsday situation in Northern Ireland. If the fears expressed here become a reality, we will have to become involved.'

I pressed him to explain why the training of Northern Irishmen by the Irish army had been terminated. He said that, because the press had got wind of what was happening, he thought it advisable to suspend it. However, as soon as it was safe to do so, it would begin again.

Blaney then said, 'These men need to make their case to Lynch. It's about time he did something.' We agreed that the meeting should take place as soon as possible. Blaney was reluctant to arrange it and asked Haughey to do so. He said, 'You'd better ring him. I can't stand the man.' Haughey picked up the telephone. As he replaced the receiver, he said, 'He will see them tomorrow morning.' We set about refining our tactics for the meeting with the Taoiseach.

Keenan was extremely tense and suggested that Lynch should be told in no uncertain terms where his responsibility lay. I was on my feet by this time and moved to Blaney's side of the table so that I could look directly at everyone in the room. I said, 'You can't walk in on the leader of a country and make demands, no matter how important or how just those demands might be.'

Gibbons agreed, and said that he was sure such an approach would be rebuffed. I explained that I believed that the best approach would be to place the facts before the man and hope that he would turn to the senior members of his cabinet for advice. 'If he does this,' I said, looking at the three men present, 'We have a commitment here, and with Boland and Ó Morain, that's five for starters.' Gibbons was enthusiastic about my suggestion. Blaney argued that some kind of commitment from the Taoiseach was vital and that he should be pressed to make the obsolete .303s available in the event of serious unrest in the North. Haughey had said nothing since his call for an invasion. I was in no doubt that he would throw in his lot with us. He had family in the North. Blaney again pressed for the .303s to be made available.

'We will ask that the weapons be held by the Irish army close to Derry so that we can be quickly armed in the event of an attack and play the rest by ear,' I said, by way of a compromise. We were not in a position to speak for Belfast. We agreed that a representative from that city should join the delegation in the morning.

'A commitment from the Taoiseach is essential,' reiterated Blaney, 'and if he won't deal with the .303s, ask him for gas masks. That's the least he can do.'

The use of gas by the police against the people of the Bogside had caused great controversy. Several doctors, including Raymond McClean in Derry, were calling for an international forum to investigate the long-term effects of exposure to the gas, with particular regard to people with respiratory problems and unborn children. It had been a long, hard day. Apart from lunchtime, Keenan and I had been under considerable pressure. Relieved, with Blaney's advice – 'get a commitment' – ringing in our ears, we left Government Buildings and headed out to spend the night in Captain Kelly's home.

Billy Kelly, the representative of the Belfast Defence Association, joined the delegation in the morning and the three of us walked in silence down the long, carpeted corridor to the Taoiseach's office. I thought of other political leaders who might have walked this same corridor. I didn't have much time for men like Cosgrave and James Dillon or their Fine Gael Party. They had never pursued the unity of the country as I would have wished. Costello had declared a truncated Republic of twenty-six counties, precipitating a reaction from the British government and strengthening the position of the loyalists. I had met Jack Lynch, the present leader, at a credit-union conference years before and hadn't been impressed. He lacked the charisma of Éamon de Valera, the founder of Fianna Fáil, or the drive of Seán Lemass, who had succeeded him.

I felt uneasy as I went in to meet Lynch. He had fluffed a chance to move closer to reunification in August 1969. He had only offered empty rhetoric and I believed that he had been outsmarted by Harold Wilson, the British Prime Minister. If Irish troops had entered Derry to stop the fighting, Ireland would have received international attention and Britain would have come under pressure to negotiate the future of Northern Ireland. My knowledge of the high-level political manoeuvrings during those frightening days, garnered from both Irish and British officers, led me to conclude that there had been an agreement that either army could move in to prevent killings in Derry. The Irish army was to hold back for as long as possible and only act if the contingent of British troops did not arrive in time. I had no doubt that both prime ministers had been in close touch during the crisis and that the agreement had forestalled any determined action by the Irish army.

'This is it,' Keenan said. The attendant knocked on the door and Lynch's voice said, 'Come in.' Lynch seemed a shy man. Some people had told me that he was weak but I didn't believe them. He had been outstanding at hurling – one of the toughest games in the world. He had been a compromise candidate during the struggle between Charles Haughey and George Colley to succeed Lemass in 1966 and had held the various factions within Fianna Fáil together. As the Taoiseach shook hands with the delegates, I noticed what I thought was a look of sadness on his face and I felt sympathy for the man who had to shoulder so much responsibility at this moment in Irish history. We discussed the situation in the North and the forthcoming report by the Scarman Tribunal. Lynch thought that he would be castigated by the tribunal for his speech on 13 August. He felt the tribunal would hold him responsible for the loyalist campaign of burnings and arson which followed his promise not to stand by.

Lynch then pointed out that, in a more recent speech in Tralee, he had gone some way towards repairing any damage he might have caused. I became worried and wondered if the look of sadness was really one of guilt. If it was, then it would be difficult to persuade him to respond positively to our request. I deferred to Keenan and the older man described once again the forces ranged against nationalists in Northern Ireland, and urged Lynch to prepare for the inevitable confrontation.

I could see Keenan was pushing too hard and suggested that guns were not necessary in Derry. Keenan took the hint and asked that the guns be stored just across the border in Donegal, so that they would be easily accessible if needed. Kelly from Belfast then took up the running. I was amazed at his approach. He demanded guns and he wanted them right in the heart of Belfast. He said that not only were the ghetto Catholics frightened, but many professional and business people were also appealing for guns.

I watched the Taoiseach flinch under the demands. I tried to calm Kelly down by returning to the situation in Derry, which was much more manageable. I asked Lynch to provide gas masks.

I made a mental note of his reply. 'Gas masks I can give you, even for humanitarian reasons, but guns I will have to think about.' The heat had gone from the discussion now, and we turned to the possibilities of political change in the long term.

I listened with dismay as the leader of the political party dedicated to the reunification of Ireland spelt out the cold economic facts: 'If we were given a gift of Northern Ireland tomorrow, we could not accept it.'

Lynch watched our reactions with large, sad eyes. 'The British government says it pumps £150 million into the Northern Ireland social services. If we were to accept responsibility for Northern Ireland, we would have to do the same so that the people would not suffer a massive drop in their living standards.' He fell silent for a moment. 'Because we could not have a country wherein the services were not equally and fairly distributed, we would have to find another £150 million to bring the social services in this country up to the same standard.' In summary, he said, 'It would require an immediate £300 million which this country has not got.'

I looked at the other two and wondered if the cold truth had registered with them. Then Lynch offered us some consolation. 'I have ordered an enquiry into the economic facts. Those may be different from that stated by Britain, but I am confident that, with our present state of economic growth, we will be able to accept responsibility for the North in ten years.' I couldn't understand the other two's jubilation outside Parliament Buildings. They were sure that Lynch had made a commitment to supply guns. I was disappointed with the way the meeting had gone and accused Kelly of frightening off Lynch: 'We blew it. That man has no intention of getting involved in Northern Ireland.'

It was the last time the Cabinet summoned Keenan and me to Dublin. Over the next few weeks, Lynch reversed the government's policy of involvement in the North and created a vacuum which the Provisional IRA was only too willing to fill.

Keenan and I were left with the task of winding up the affairs of the Derry Citizens' Defence Association. That basically meant clearing an outstanding debt of about £600. Keenan arranged a meeting with a civil-rights group in London through his old comrade-in-arms Seán MacDermott, and he and I flew over. The meeting was held in a pub and, after an informal presentation of accounts, they readily agreed to help us. We got down to the more serious business of drinking and discussing Irish affairs. Knowing that I was looking for a job, MacDermott introduced me to a friend who was a subcontractor for George Wimpey and Company, the civil-engineering firm. While the rest of them discussed politics and their exploits for the cause, my new acquaintance and I slowly unwound, enjoying the company and watching Keenan impress everyone with his analysis of the political situation in the North. The two of us had had a happy association and each of us seemed to fulfil the needs and make up for weaknesses of the other. Keenan's idealism and dedication and my own pragmatism and organisational ability had perfectly complemented each other. Keenan had already begun making plans to continue the struggle, which was his life's work, while I was trying to pick up the threads of my life again after the convulsions of the last year. I smiled as Keenan, reminiscing on recent events, jokingly referred to me as 'the most devious bastard' he had ever had the privilege of working with. That night we slept in MacDermott's home and returned to Derry next day.

Three days later, an application form for employment with Wimpey arrived in the post. I completed it and posted it the same day. Two days later I was invited to come to London for an interview. The tall concrete and glass building bearing the name WIMPEY towered over the Borough of Hammersmith. I walked towards it from the tube station. As I sat in the public office, I got a flavour of the Wimpey empire: men were coming from and going to Saudi Arabia, Trinidad and a dozen other exotic countries. I read a company brochure: £500 million of assets. There was a sense of urgency and power about the place which was distinctly English, although most of the accents were Irish. My thoughts again turned to the strange love/hate relationship between England and Ireland. Irish soldiers, clerics and builders had all contributed to England's power and prestige, and now I had joined the queue.

A man called McDonald sat behind the desk in the personnel office, cutting thin slivers from a large plug of tobacco. He nodded to a chair. Rubbing the tobacco between his hands, he began filling the large bowl of a curled pipe. I warmed to the man. His big head was covered with a shock of unruly hair turning grey, his eyes were bright and his face was craggy. His hands fascinated me. I had expected a personnel manager to wear cuff links and have manicured nails, not to be crushing tobacco with big horny hands. Promotion had not erased the marks of years on building sites: office work had not softened the well-chiselled fingers or removed the knotted veins forced to the surface of the skin by years of hard work. The ritual of filling the pipe over, he rose and shook me by the hand. 'You've had a hell of a time,' he said, and, sitting down again, he relit the pipe. His informality put me at my ease. Soon the big man from Mayo was telling me about the War of Independence, during which he had spent a night in prison after reciting a poem in Irish at a public meeting in Ballina. Suddenly he got to his feet and relived his defiance of the British occupation of Ireland, his voice filling the room. All activity in the adjoining offices ceased as the seditious verse reverberated through the thin, glazed partitions.

Not once during the strange interview did he question my capabilities or examine my experience, although my application file lay open on the desk. An hour or so later, I was sent for a medical examination. The doctor also turned out to be Irish. On my return to the office, I was told that I was to be sent to the Caribbean in a week's time. 'It's much more pleasant there than in the Middle East,' said McDonald as we shook hands.

Back in Derry, I began tying up various loose ends, as my contract was for fifteen months. I had no money at the time. I phoned John Nicholl, who readily agreed to supply oil for the central-heating system. I would pay him back when my circumstances changed. I went to see Brendan McGonigle at the AIB Bank. Could he honour any further expenditure on top of my existing large overdraft?

McGonigle looked at me and said, 'I have never looked at your account, and I never will. Sign whatever cheques you need.'

In the middle of the week, Canavan invited me to dinner in Moville. I went to what turned out to be a farewell party in my honour. Most of the members of the Citizens' Defence Association were there. Keenan made a presentation to me. As we shook hands, I knew that the grand alliance was over.

I had one more thing to do. I went to the shop owned by Louis McCafferty, the man who had paid the fine for the boy who had robbed him the year before. As I entered the shop, I was not discouraged by the greeting I received. Small talk over, I asked: 'Did the woman ever pay the bill she owed you?' Louis took a large book from beneath the counter, opened it and, running his finger down the entries, checking them against dates, said to me: 'She only missed Christmas week and owes me just two payments.'

My faith in the woman and her family vindicated, I was as pleased as on the day Haughey offered £5,000 to help the Defence Association. I had mixed feelings about leaving the country. I needed the work but, more importantly, I needed time to think. I believed that the peace between the authorities and the nationalist population of the North would inevitably break down and create confrontation on the streets, and I was uneasy about leaving. I discussed my ambivalence with my eldest son, John, who said, 'The people have been awakened and the demand for civil rights will give way to a demand for ancient rights. You will be no good the next time; the people will need a man who can kill.'

POSTSCRIPT

WHY?

Eoghan, son of Niall of the Nine Hostages, came north and founded his castle at Grianan, the ancient site on the hill of Aileach, five miles from the Isle of Derry. From Niall descended the two great families of O'Donnell and O'Neill. In 546 AD, the Christian monk Colmcille, a direct descendant of Niall, built his monastic settlement on the Isle of Derry. Symbolically separating the druidic past and the age of Christianity, Colmcille burned down the oak grove which had been sacred to the druids, taking great care to protect all the other oaks on the island. To emphasise the break with the past, he blessed a well which supplied water for fighting fires. From 546 until 1568, when the gunpowder stored by English forces in the great church of Temple Mor exploded and destroyed the monastic city, there was a continuous ecclesiastical presence on the Isle of Derry.

The northern territories of the O'Neills and the O'Donnells were separated by the Inishowen peninsula, which was claimed by both families. The O'Neills claimed it by right of heritage, the O'Donnells by right of conquest. Until the coming of the Norman De Burghs in the late thirteenth century, the peninsula was under the stewardship of the McLaughlins. They were relatives of the O'Neills, and a distinguished family in their own right, although in decline. In 1333, after a brief but violent incursion into the north-west by the De Burghs, the O'Dochartaigh family, a sub-sept of the O'Donnells, filled the ensuing power vacuum in Inishowen. Between 1333 and 1608, the

O'Dochartaighs held on to their land by paying tithes to the O'Donnells or to the O'Neills, depending on which family was strongest at any given time. Under their stewardship the land was improved and the people prospered, often in difficult circumstances: every new generation of O'Donnells and O'Neills contested the overlordship of the north of Ireland and forced the O'Dochartaighs to be prepared for war at all times. Continually mediating between the two great families, the O'Dochartaighs became practised diplomats. In the fifteenth century, on land granted them by the McLaughlins, the O'Dochartaighs built a castle on the Isle of Derry. When Elizabeth I decided to conquer the north of Ireland in 1600, her general, Dowcra, occupied Derry and the O'Dochartaigh castle. He used the stones from the derelict monastic settlement to build a walled city. The castle would later serve as a magazine during the siege of Derry in 1689.

In 1603, after the Battle of Kinsale, the heads of the O'Donnell and O'Neill clans fled to Spain, and their power over the north of Ireland ended. The O'Dochartaighs remained lords of Inishowen until the death of their chieftain, Cahir, at the Battle of Kilmacrennan in 1608. The defeat of the O'Dochartaighs heralded the collapse of the Gaelic order, which had endured for more than 2,000 years. After the defeat of the O'Dochartaigh clan, Chichester, the Lord Lieutenant of Ireland, who had long been envious of the rich lands of the O'Dochartaighs with their herds of cattle and rivers teeming with salmon, hurried northward from Dublin to seize Inishowen. Lest he be accused of stealth, he hastily legalised his conquest of Inishowen. It was not the first time that the English had changed the law to legitimise their actions in Ireland, and it certainly would not be the last. Having annexed the land, Chichester ordered that 600 of the finest O'Dochartaigh fighting men be sent to fight for the Protestant King of Sweden. Tradition has it that, before their departure in chains, knives were used on them so that they would never sire children who might one day rebel against England. To avoid capture, many families retreated into the mountains of central Inishowen. A great number of men fled towards the south-west – some eventually took ship to Europe, to join the armies of France and Spain. Cahir O'Dochartaigh's family fled first to the safe haven provided by relatives in Cavan, and then moved on. After a harrowing journey, they landed in Spain. Over the years, some trickled back to join their families and work as labourers on land they once owned. Most never returned, but a longing for home was transmitted from one generation to the next. For a time, the once-great clan, was in danger of dying out. The large families produced by succeeding generations made good the losses of the seventeenth century. The new owners of Inishowen were known as planters. They built gracious houses and sent their children to England for their education. They anglicised the place names and family names, so that Inis Eoghan became Inishowen and O'Dochartaigh became Doherty.

It is in the marrow of the bone.

INDEX

O'Neill, Terence, 64-5, 83, 84-5, 91-2, 101, 102-3, 167
calls election under pressure, 97
Observer, The, 86
Orange Order, the (Orangemen), 24, 38, 110-1, 124
Orme, Stanley, 146, 147, 149

Paisley, Ian, 52, 91, 95, 101, 112, 179
organises demonstration in Armagh, 83
addresses meeting in Guildhall, 85
Patton, John, 27, 104
pawnbrokers, 20
Pennyburn Credit Union, 47
People's Democracy, 84
ambush on People's Democracy at Burntollet Bridge, 88-9
Philbin, Bishop, 215
Porter, Robert, 103, 105, 132, 206-7
Potsdam Courier the, 186, 217

Queen's University, Belfast, 31, 40, 41

refugees, 182-3
Reynolds, Major Mike, 156, 197, 210
RUC (Royal Ulster Constabulary), 55-8, 60, 61, 65, 72, 80, 83, 84, 95, 106-9, 145, 148, 149, 152, 155, 161, 185, 207, 214, 216, 217-8

Saor Éire, 179-80, 199
Scarman, Sir Leslie, 207
Scarman Tribunal, 207-9, 225
Seth, Louden, 161, 162
Siege of Derry, 37-8
Sinclair, Betty, 55, 80
Sinn Féin 124-5, 190
Special Powers Act, 24, 47-8, 105, 214

Tarleton, Peter, 159
Taylor, Sergeant, 84
Tenants' Association, 215, 217
Territorial Army, the, 24
Todd, Lieutenant Colonel, 148-9, 152, 143, 155-6, 163
tuberculosis (consumption), 19
Twohig, Father, 157

Unionist Party, the, 28, 33-4, 35, 50, 59, 100, 120-1
university controversy, 40-3

Walker, Governor, 37, 38
West, Harry, 91
Wilson, Harold, 138, 224
Wilton, Claude, 62, 63, 100, 132
women in Derry, 20-1

Young Socialists, the, 159
Young, Sir Arthur, 214

HANDING OVER RECEIPT

No. .... Rank ..TPR.............

Name ....M^cGARRIGLE, also..........

Coy, Bty, Sqn, etc...........Tommy LAIRD...........

Corps/Regt. ....Q. R. 1. H.:...........

Unit..

I was Guard Commander on ..27. AUG..........

..1969.......... when at ....hrs

the above named Soldier/N.C.O. was handed over to ....

to be detained by ....Tа...........................

..........R.M.P...........................of the R.M.P.

Signed ....Sgt SWABY...........

Unit ....24 BDE Pro Unit...........

....

No. .... Rank............

Date ..27 AUG 69...........

The receipt given to me by the British Army after we handed over a soldier
captured in Free Derry (see p 201)